D0477935

GUIDE TO THE
QUAKER PARROT

Mattie Sue Athan

With 98 photographs
Illustrations by Michele Earle-Bridges

BARRON'S

Dedication
for Philip

Acknowledgments
With special thanks to Susan Green, Gale Whittington, David Wright, Art Freud, Dr. Matthew Vriends, Josoph DeAlmaioa, Dr. Steven Feldman, Dr. Jerry LaBonde, Dr. Greg Harrison, Dr. Margaret Gaut, Dianalee Deter, Sally Blanchard, Joe Southern, Barb and Gary Steffens and their quaker friends, Jim and Patty Hannigan, Joanne Davis, Robert Dominguez, Kathy Kullback, Brendan Kullback, David Kullback, Karen Goodman, Chris Davis, Dr. Irene Pepperberg, Carol D'Arizo, Julia Murad, Sharon Silvas, Vera Herst, my family and clients, and, of course, Tza-tza the Wonderquaker. This book, like my first, would never have been written without the influence of Phil Price and Bessie Cutcher.

About the Author
Mattie Sue Athan has studied the behavior of companion and feral quaker parrots in North America since 1978. Her specific work as a companion parrot behavior consultant takes her into the homes of concerned owners of misbehaving quakers. She often assists in the recovery of flown-away quakers.

About the Photographer
Susan Green is a well-known photographer of companion animals. Her work has appeared in several Barron's Educational Series books as well as *Positively Pets*, *American Cage Bird Magazine*, and numerous other specialty publications.

Please note: *Poorly socialized or unhealthy quaker parrots may be a danger to the well-being of humans in the household. Escaped companion quakers could represent an environmental threat in some places. Outdoor release or unrestricted outdoor flight of quaker parrots is absolutely condemned by the ethical quaker owner. This book recommends that quaker parrot wing feathers be carefully trimmed at least three times yearly.*

Photo Credits
Lisa Lalone: page 2; Mattie Sue Athan: page 81; all other photos by Susan Green.

All inquiries should be addressed to:
Barron's Educational Series, Inc.
250 Wireless Boulevard
Hauppauge, New York 11788

International Standard Book No. 0-7641-0176-5

Library of Congress Catalog Card No. 97-8730

Library of Congress Cataloging-in-Publication Data

Athan, Mattie Sue.
    Complete guide to the companion quaker parrot / Mattie Sue Athan.
        p.   cm.
    Includes bibliographical references and index.
    ISBN 0-7641-0176-5
    1. Monk parakeet. I. Title.
SF473.M6A84   1997
636.6′865—dc21   97-8730
                                                          CIP

Printed in Hong Kong

9876

Contents

Preface

Sometimes a book evolves from the imagination of the writer. Sometimes it's hatched because there is obvious need for the information it provides. This book is a combination of both with an accent on the latter. As a matter of fact, there has seldom been a greater need for a bird book than there is for this one. The quaker parrot is hated and feared outdoors as a result of an only partially deserved reputation as an agricultural pest. It is also sometimes hated and feared indoors for its reputation as an aggressive little tyrant.

Many people love the quaker parrot. In a dozen and a half years of "field research" in living rooms shared with quakers, I've seen many very charming birds. I consider the hand-fed quaker parrot to be the *only* bird that is virtually guaranteed to acquire human speech; however, even among quaker lovers, there is widespread concern about their suitability as companions.

I was surprised to learn that David Wright, a well-known quaker lover and author of many articles on feral quakers, did not recommend the quaker parrot as a first bird, especially around children. At first, I could not believe that someone who loves quakers would say such derogatory things about them, but, upon reflection, I had to agree that untrained quakers can be dangerous to children and may not be the best choice as a first bird.

On the other hand, I've known very many beloved quakers who were not only first birds, but also lived with children who expected to interact with them. The difference between David Wright's observations (which are valid) and my observations (which are also valid) is the reason for this book.

A well-socialized quaker can be an adorable and fascinating companion, but a quaker is not exactly a pet. Even the best socialized individual may have occasional "temper tantrums." This is a factor of the birds' wild nature and a part of their

The quaker parrot is considered an opportunistic agricultural pest in its native Argentina.

joy to be with and are well suited to living with children (presuming the children can also be trained).

I would like to thank all those who contributed to this project's development: members of the quaker-loving community who asked for the book; my local Denver support group, family, friends, and clients who were neglected during its writing; and the folks at Barron's for their constant support.

Especially, I'd like to thank Vera Herst for her tireless assistance and Sharon Silvas, publisher of *Colorado Woman News,* for misquoting me. Once, Sharon asked if I was working on a book, and I replied, "Yes, I'm working on a book on the quaker parrot." A *Colorado Woman News* article later reported that I was working on a book on "...efforts to save the quaker parrot."

charm. They are little feathered dragons, and sometimes they must be allowed to breathe a little fire.

A poorly socialized quaker can be a flying feathered disaster looking for a place to happen. The difference between the dream bird and the nightmare harpy is appropriate socialization for life in the human living room. The techniques described in this book usually produce cooperative, interactive birds that are a

The well-socialized quaker parrot is a treasured companion.

Maybe *this is* such a book. In a world of increasing human population and expanding agriculture to feed those hungry humans, the quaker parrot is considered an unwelcome pest in its native range. The bird is an anachronism, an obsolete organism that apparently no longer has a place in the "natural" scheme of things. At this writing, it is illegal to own or to sell quaker parrots in ten states. Our living rooms may be the only places in the world where the quaker parrot is truly welcome. Let's work to ensure that these delightful little dinosaurs can adjust to the physical and behavioral habitats in human homes— who knows how long they will be tolerated outdoors.

Chapter One
Bird of Paradox

The Plain Bird with the Colorful Personality

Once before I had come to evaluate an African gray who never quite fit into this particular human flock. Now I was here to see a yellow-naped Amazon, the new third bird in the home. But the family's first love—and favorite companion bird—was a common quaker parrot.

"Why didn't anyone tell us that the quaker was the perfect parrot?" they asked me more than once.

They'd heard such wonderful things about African grays and Amazons, and such terrible things about quakers that they thought they were missing something. Their two large-bird experiences only reinforced how wonderful their quaker was. He talked with understanding, learned new things all the time, stepped up for anybody (away from his cage), and, after ten years in the home, he was still finding new ways to amuse his human family.

I'd heard stories like this before: Quaker parrot owners may be disappointed with larger birds even though the larger birds were purchased because they were said to be "better" than quakers. But, occasionally, I happen upon someone who's seen groups of quakers, maybe imported or breeding birds, saying, "I don't like quakers."

And I might hear someone who has known maybe two or three quakers (and sometimes even someone who wouldn't recognize a quaker) repeat those same words: "I don't like quakers."

It doesn't even sound like that first family and those subsequent "somebodies" are talking about the

The quaker parrot is considered by some to be the "perfect" parrot.

Baby quakers are not born with behavior problems, but they can learn or develop such problems quickly.

feathered monk(ey)s are called "the poor man's yellow nape." In terms of price, size, temperament, talking ability, and accessibility, hand-fed domestic monks are everything one could expect of a companion parrot.

My own quaker—who receives minimal attention in this home of many pets—is an amazingly astute conversationalist. Tza-tza likes to talk on the phone (although he can't figure out how to get the phone to answer without my help). When I have one of my asthma attacks, he coughs along, then asks, "Are you OK?"

Tza-tza bathes daily, then I have to change his water again or he drinks bathwater all day. He even taught himself to groom his own nails by blunt filing them on the rough bars of his wrought iron cage.

Quaker parrots are well appreciated in the pet trade. Gale Whittington, owner of Colorado Seed and Pet (a 45-year-old bird store), says, "The quaker is extremely hardy and one of the best talkers. I sell more quakers than any other small parrot."

Description and Origin of Name

Quaker parrots are bright green with a gray cowl across the head, lighter gray cheeks, and scalloped markings on the upper chest. Some have a wash of yellow ochre across the belly. Although resembling conures, quakers are the lone members of their genus. There are four subspecies: *M. m. monachus, M. m. calita, M. m. cotorra*, and

same bird! There must be a tremendous difference between the nice and the not-so-nice quakers, for no other type of parrot seems to inspire such vehement and opposite opinions. The quaker is truly the most loved *and abhorred* parrot.

An unsocialized quaker can be a very unpleasant animal, but hand-fed baby quakers don't come into this world unpleasant. Why then, do so many of them end up that way? Nature has something to do with it, but poor patterning and a poorly planned environment are often the culprits here. A quaker doesn't have to always be a little tyrant, for these birds are very predictable and respond dependably to common behavioral techniques.

In *Myiopsitta monachus,* the common monk or quaker parrot, I see all the mimicking ability of the budgie, African gray, and yellow-naped Amazon in a sturdy, easily manageable size. Indeed, in some places, these little gray-cowled

M. m. luchsi. They are of South American origin, but they have established feral populations in numerous other locales. The quaker parrot is commonly kept as a pet in many countries. Lutino (yellow) and blue mutations have been developed in captivity, but they remain rare and expensive. There are no human-observable physical gender characteristics.

Certainly, the name, "monk" is derived from this bird's drab colors and the cowl shape of the marking on the head, but, there remains disagreement today over the source of the common name, "quaker" parrot. Those who first see an adult bird often believe that the name comes from the plainness of the bird's attire. The gray cowl and face, and modest scalloped markings on the bird's chest are not unlike the plain and modest attire of the Society of Friends, religious humans also sometimes called "Quakers."

Those who have seen this bird as an infant are often convinced that it is called "quaker" after one of its neonatal behaviors: Babies exhibit a sort of "palsied" response when feeding and begging. This quaking behavior differs from the gulping motions of other baby parrots and may also indicate the bird's status to other members of the flock. Some quaker parrots retain this body language longer than others; some revert to it occasionally when they are courting, ill, or otherwise needy.

While I may use the terms quaker and monk interchangeably, I don't

Because of the quaker parrot's long, graduated tail, it may be accurately called either a parakeet or a parrot.

usually call this bird a "parakeet." Many people use the term parakeet because of the bird's long tail, but I believe that this word can be too easily misinterpreted to mean that the quaker is a tiny, docile bird like a budgie. Nothing could be further from the truth. This little hookbill has all the spit and vinegar of its larger

The baby quaker parrot doing its thing.

Parts of the quaker parrot.
1. Cere
2. Forehead
3. Eye ring
4. Iris
5. Ear coverts
6. Back of head
7. Nape of neck
8. Bend of wing
9. Mantle
10. Back
11. Median wing coverts
12. Greater wing coverts
13. Secondaries
14. Primaries
15. Tail
16. Upper mandible
17. Lower mandible
18. Breast
19. Abdomen
20. Foot

cousins. Because of its strong resemblance to the two other families of long-tailed New World parrots—conures and macaws—I prefer to call *Myiopsitta monachus* a parrot in this book.

A parrot must be allowed to kiss only a clean, closed mouth to protect it from hostile microbes in human saliva.

Personality Traits

Highly social and eager to please (as well as dominate), domestic baby quakers usually love to be cuddled. Some birds never learn to step up (see Step-up Practice, pages 17–18) because they like to be picked up like a baseball (with the palm around the back).

Baby quakers are often fond of kissing and sometimes can be trusted to give tender nibbles rather than painful nips. But they must be allowed to kiss only a clean, closed mouth to protect them from hostile microbes in human saliva.

Their talking (and noisemaking) capacity is legend. Hand-fed domestic quakers often rival African grays in their ability to acquire huge vocabularies. Most quaker parrots also learn

4

to talk more quickly than most African grays. Hand-fed domestics seldom develop the calls of their imported predecessors who had a loud, raucous "cultural" language. Wild quaker sounds can be so repugnant that interlopers flee just so they don't have to hear the noise. On the other hand, wild quakers are sometimes tolerant, even accepting, of the presence of certain other species in their huge communal nests.

Companion quakers are also quite African gray-like in their tendency to bond strongly to one person or location, so controls must be maintained to minimize this tendency to develop territory-related aggression. We see few significant behavior problems in domestic quakers with a diverse environment including a large assortment of well-used, frequently rotated toys. If adequate behavioral and environmental controls are maintained to prevent the development of aggression, domestic hand-fed quakers can be outstanding companions. As several of my clients have discovered, they might even be "better" (in some situations) than some of their larger, more-famous cousins!

Although escaped quakers continue to be politically demonized by agricultural interests—being illegal in ten states—feral quakers have not lived up to their pernicious reputation. This bird's presence in the eastern United States has been reported in *A Field Guide to Eastern Birds* (sponsored by the National Audubon Society and the National

Quaker parrots are very predictable and dependably respond to common behavioral techniques.

Wildlife Federation) since 1964. By 1980 this publication had observed that after years of unsuccessful attempts to nest, the quaker "...probably will not become established."[*] Since these birds have not been imported since 1992, and since only wild-hatched birds have the ability to survive wild; the quaker parrot will almost certainly fail to proliferate in the United States.

---

[*] Peterson, Roger Tory. *Peterson Field Guides to Eastern Birds*. Houghton Mifflin Company, 1980, page 178. "Monk Parakeet" text from *A Field Guide to Eastern Birds*. Copyright © 1980 by Roger Tory Peterson. Reprinted by permission of Houghton Mifflin Company. All rights reserved.

Control and Other Issues

A smart little quaker parrot might prove extremely innovative in trying to control *everything* in the social environment. For example, a companion quaker might try to dominate the environment with its voice, a well-socialized quaker would know to attack or chat with its toys, a quiet companion quaker might require more toys than other types of parrots. (Of course, almost anything can be considered a "toy.")

Unlike a "normal" (cavity-breeding) parrot obsessed with dismantling everything it can get its beak on, the quaker often actually plays with its toys. A quaker parrot will remove the toys from the cage and will sometimes dismantle them, but this nest-building parrot will not usually destroy the components of the toy as many cavity-breeding parrots do. The bird may use the toys as tools,

Quaker parrots are less destructive than their larger, cavity-breeding cousins.

especially for personal pleasure, but an adult quaker will be especially motivated to control *where* the toys are placed. More specifically, the quaker wants to arrange things. Like a cat's interest in catnip, this behavior develops as the bird matures.

The first home where I encountered a quaker parrot was a three-person/three-parrot family. Mom had a baby blue-fronted Amazon, Dad had a shy, doting lilac-crowned Amazon, and the teenage daughter had an independent little quaker that would go crazy when anyone touched its cage. The family didn't consider this a problem since the bird was absolutely darling away from the cage.

The cage contained a couple of dozen toys including a little wire Chinese puzzle hanging from a chain. The girl would spend 15 to 20 seconds hooking the paper clip-like device to the cage bar. The bird would rush over to the misplaced toy (expending the famous quaker curse), grab the puzzle, and, in less time than it took the girl to put the puzzle together, unhook it, administering a punishing "bop" before marching proudly away, fussing all the time.

If the humans moved a plastic ladder from one side of the cage to another (there was barely room to move anything inside the crowded cage), the little bird rushed to pull and push and tug the ladder immediately back to its appointed place.

This incredible need to control object placement in the immediate

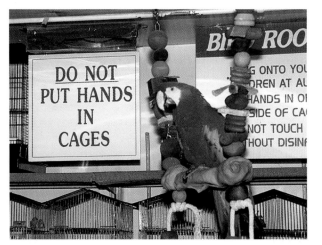

environment is more developed in the quaker than in other, especially larger, parrots whose primary instincts involve removing objects from cavities. This instinct to arrange things is probably related to the bird's unusual wild nesting habits. Quakers aren't usually compulsive "chain saws" like their cavity-breeding cousins. The instinct to arrange rather than destroy probably occurs because the quakers are nest-building parrots, a little quirk that makes several elements of behavior modification different for quakers than for other parrots. It also makes the quaker parrot an ideal choice for someone who has antiques and valuable fine art that might be quickly decimated by a cockatoo or macaw.

Hand-fed quakers enjoy a well-deserved reputation as talkers that rivals African grays and yellow napes. Actually, a good-talking quaker parrot usually develops a larger vocabulary than either the African gray or yellow nape, but the words are seldom as understandable as those spoken by the two larger types of parrots.

Quaker parrots are a great dollar value for one who likes a little more spunk than a cockatiel without the problems accompanying many larger hookbills. They may be noisy in multiples, especially if the flock includes wild-hatched or parent-raised birds. A single quaker is an excellent pet for an adolescent, teen, or adult with limited space and resources. Actually, quaker parrots probably achieve their best companion characteristics when kept as an only bird—they are unquestionably better companions as only quakers.

Behaviorally, I find the quaker more predictable than brotegeris, conures, Amazons, cockatoos, or grays. They can be nippy in and around the cage, but are often quite docile away from the cage. Quaker parrots usually respond easily, quickly, and positively to the techniques described here.

Quaker Culture: Who Goes Where?

No other parrot lives and breeds in such close proximity to others of its own and other species as the wild quaker parrot. In its native range this colony-breeding creature shares its constructed nests not only with many other quakers, but also with other species such as bats, geese, and opossums.[*]

While wild quaker parrots allow these neighbors to literally walk across their "front porch," captive quakers are famous for developing territorial-related aggression, allowing no one even near their cage. I call this "the quaker paradox." How does an animal that is so tolerant of close side-by-side activity in the wild become so intolerant of others in its indoor territory?

---

[*] Matthew M. Vriends, Ph.D., telephone interview, 1992.

First, let's look at who goes where in outdoor quaker society. The three-room quaker condo could be likened to an apartment (in a building of many apartments) with a bedroom, a living room, and a front porch. Different individual members of a quaker's group are allowed to enter different levels of the quaker's personal quarters. Mom, eggs, newly hatched babies, and possibly Dad are allowed in the bedroom. Older juvenile chicks and Dad are allowed in the living room. Neighbors, including, presumably, parents, grown offspring, cousins, in-laws, and other colony regulars can walk across the front porch.

How does the wild quaker parrot know who has the right to be where in this complex social hierarchy? How does a quaker recognize different individuals in the group? How does a quaker recognize an intruder?

While some of this information is probably conveyed by language, I believe the first, most obvious way a quaker can tell who's who in quaker society is by observing the individual's posture or body language. Baby quakers have a signaling behavior that they are, indeed, babies—that is, they quake. This is not like regular conure head bobbing; it more resembles the human condition palsy. A couple of years ago, I mentioned this behavior to a CompuServe correspondent who was expecting her first baby quaker. She had hand-fed many baby conures, and when I mentioned the quaking of the babies, she smiled—in computer language,

that's :-)—and said, "Of course, all baby conures bob and gulp and beg when feeding."

I replied that quakers were different. I heard nothing back for a few days.

On the third day, I received a long e-mail thank-you note. The lady graciously assured me that she would have presumed the bird ill if she had not been forewarned about the quaking behavior. "I never saw a bird do anything like that before!" she said.

I believe this quaking behavior in juvenile birds may be the way the parents know who is still allowed in the living room and who is to be pushed to the porch and outdoors. In like fashion, I believe the behavior of individuals in close proximity probably signals the residents how to respond to those individuals. If the neighbor is on its way home to feed its family and walks resolutely across the front porch—giving no eye contact, showing no fear—the resident adult quaker will probably do no more than fuss or cuss briefly as the neighbor walks by. If, on the other hand, the neighbor is actually an interloper that makes eye contact, then quits eye contact, moves fast, shows fear, and/or retreats, the resident *knows* that the individual is *not* entitled to be there. The chase is on!

This interaction is probably the source of another important quaker behavior. Especially in the vicinity of the cage, an adult quaker might chase anything, regardless of size, that moves in the opposite direction. It's as though each little quaker had the motto tattooed on its heart: "If you run, I'll chase you."

Interactions with Humans

I believe that interactions with humans—especially humans who don't understand how they're supposed to behave in "quaker society"—can reinforce the companion quaker's natural instinct to chase any shy or unsure creature away from its territory. Some quakers express this chasing behavior quite violently. Empathy, concern, and fear—all appropriate—fuel human behavior here. Repeating this interaction establishes chasing as a habit or pattern that is then frequently expressed and expanded. If an intruder has been identified and fails to retreat, there may be a very loud and intense battle, and the intruder will be convinced to leave.

Chasing and Territorialism

Avoid the development of chasing and territorialism around the cage by training both the baby parrot and all humans interacting with the baby parrot in mutually supportive behaviors. If the bird's cage is 5 to 6 cubic feet (1.5–1.8 cu m) or less, we might consider that the entire cage is the apartment. The bedroom might occupy the space where the bird sleeps and cuddles with the favorite cuddling toy, the living room might be the rest of the cage, and the front porch might be the top of the cage or the top of the cage door. With a larger cage, a

A quaker parrot allowed to learn chasing behaviors may attack human feet.

flight, or walk-in cage only a portion of the cage might be the apartment.

I believe that the primary human/quaker relationship best resembles the relationship that the bird would have with a parent, not a mate. Anthropomorphizing just a bit here, human relationship counselors tell us that domestic abuse within couples can usually be stopped immediately by the arrival of an outsider, especially, the parent of either member of the couple. Adult individuals within a couple usually develop both *more intimate* and *more adversarial* relationships with their spouses than with their parents and in-laws.

One or two humans might expect to maintain a relationship of sufficient closeness with the companion quaker parrot to be likened to a parent/child relationship. The parent of an adult bird might be welcome in the living room, but would probably never enter the adult bird's bedroom.

Our living rooms may be the only places in the world where quaker parrots are truly welcome.

the cage is probably the most influential factor in how the bird responds to that individual. Insecurity or fearfulness—especially if accompanied by retreating—will pattern the bird to chasing behavior that can become violent in the future.

In the interest of balanced relationships with multiple individuals, a companion quaker is best frequently reinforced to step up from the front porch (the cage top or cage door) rather than from inside the living room, which might be reserved for only the most intimate friend. Step-up practice (see pages 17–19 and 27–28), including use of eye contact, the Wobble Correction (see page 21), and Good Hand/Bad Hand (see page 24), is just as significant in the effective training of human handlers as it is in the effective training of the quaker parrot. If everyone is trained to handle the bird with the same self-confident, sensitive, and predictable mannerisms, the bird's responses will usually remain cooperative and predictable with most, if not all, trained humans.

Most humans interacting with the companion quaker can probably be compared to flockmates. Most humans are, therefore, best taught to expect the bird to step up peacefully and cooperatively from the front porch. One or two favorite or primary humans might require the bird to step up from inside the cage (the living room), but the quaker parrot benefits from being allowed to have a little private sanctuary where it sleeps or cuddles (the bedroom).

The behavior of an individual expecting to interact with a quaker at

Chapter Two
The New Baby Quaker

Selecting and Purchasing the Premium Baby Quaker Parrot

Hand-feeding disasters can be devastating, especially to the bird; therefore, I believe that quaker parrots are best professionally hand-fed and weaned. One might select a baby being hand-fed, then visit periodically to cuddle and begin socializing the bird before it comes home.

Karen Goodman, owner of the African Gray, a Colorado bird store, reports that in months when they are available (usually spring and fall), she sells more quakers than cockatiels. "Because of their price and talking ability, quakers are the best deal around. The domestic handfeds are quite different from the imports we were seeing a few years ago—less noisy, more talkative and cuddly.

Kathy Kullback, an employee of the African Gray, says, "While quaker parrots are abundant some years, their availability can be very limited other years. That means that sometimes baby quakers will cost $200 and sometimes they will cost $500."

Premium-quality hand-fed babies may be available seasonally. Ask dependable locals about when the best babies are available in your area. Often, baby birds are less expensive and there is a larger number of babies to choose from in the spring rather than around gift-giving season in the winter.

Quaker prices in the United States usually range from under $50 for older resale imports to over

Baby quaker parrots should be professionally hand-fed and weaned.

Observe reasonable health protocol when shopping for a baby quaker parrot.

$200 for hand-fed baby domestics. Look for a breeder or dealer with a reputation for healthy, well-adjusted birds and with a reputation for taking care of things if anything is amiss. Some breeders and dealers who have been in business for years offer little service after the sale; they may specialize in the "inexpensive" quaker. Other long-term breeders or dealers may be well known for servicing the sale—providing backup care information and other valuable help, such as, perhaps, free grooming, even years after the bird was sold.

I believe that most people can access the most desirable companion characteristics by having only one quaker per household. If the bird relates to humans as parents and leaders of the flock, it is less likely to learn wild quaker parrot behaviors that can be less than charming.

Young quaker parrots are easy to recognize. They have a soft beak, especially on the sides at the lower mandible, more green and less gray on the hood, and less pronounced barring on the breast. A young bird frequently pulls its head to the back of its neck and "quakes" when it wants attention. This behavior mimics the feeding response needed to quickly ingest the masticated food being dispensed by their busy parents.

Baby quakers don't have fully developed immune systems. When shopping for a baby quaker, be sure to visit only one breeder or dealer each day. Bathe, change clothing, and shoes before visiting each facility. Many facilities will require you to wash your hands before handling their babies. Be sure to ask permission to handle baby birds, as some caring dealers allow babies to be handled only with supervision. This protects the baby (and the interests of future owners) from mishaps involving mishandling at an early age.

The Noisy or Quiet Quaker Parrot

Many elements of the quaker parrot's language are far from pleasant. If you wish a quiet bird, seek a baby that was not raised around noisy imported or breeding groups of quakers. This is tremendously important. Many quaker breeders have a proven track record of consistently providing quiet, talkative quakers, while some breeders don't have a clue about how to produce a quaker parrot that isn't noisy. Be sure to research the expected characteristics of your new baby quaker by talking with other people who know or own babies from the same source.

If acquiring human speech is important, ask the hand-feeder which babies are already talking, for many baby quakers will acquire a few human words before they are weaned. Look for an active baby that is easily calmed with soothing words or for a calm baby that is easily excited by a new toy or flirtation. Look for a bright-eyed, alert bird that is interested in what you do. Look for a dealer who is willing to give a reasonable guarantee of the bird's health.

Gender

I consider gender to be irrelevant in the area of speech capability, but it may affect disposition. Now that gender can be safely and easily determined with DNA sexing, many quaker breeders and dealers have their babies sexed before selling them. This involves the removal of one drop of blood from a toenail, and sending it in a kit to a laboratory for analysis.* Barb Steffens, co-owner of Wings and Things in Arvada, Colorado, has her baby quakers DNA-sexed on request and observes that the hens seem nippier. I cannot confirm her observation because I have known so many quakers without knowing their gen-

* Zoogen, Incorporated, United States 1-800-995-BIRD, Canada 1.519.837.BIRD, Europe/UK 44.0962.880376.

ders, but I can confirm similar observations in budgies, lovebirds, and eclectus.

Territorialism

If the quaker hen is the primary guardian of who comes and goes to the backroom of the family condo, that might translate into a more territorial hen. There is, however, great variation between one bird and another, and a male quaker that has been patterned to chase and defend will be just as fierce as a female one. A female bird that has been appropriately patterned for cooperation will be as sweet as an appropriately patterned male bird. The effects of territorialism in either male or female quaker parrots must be mitigated with good behavioral practice and much handling and socialization out of sight of the cage. The primary area where humans interact with the companion quaker should remain, for the bird's lifetime, out of sight of the cage.

Weaning

When purchasing a baby quaker and waiting for it to wean, it's a good idea to visit the baby and handle it at least once weekly. Resist the temptation to ask that weaning be hurried along. Look for a dealer who lets the baby birds set their own pace for weaning. This technique, sometimes called, "abundance weaning" will produce a more independent, confident bird that stays tame.

I don't consider a quaker parrot fully weaned until it can crack seed.

Even if we don't intend to feed seed in the future, unless the bird can use the beak and tongue well enough to crack seed, I believe other chewing-related problems could develop in the future.

A parrot of any kind is a long-term commitment and must not be an impulse purchase. If you buy one while on vacation, be sure quaker parrots are legal in your home state before taking one home. (See page 111.)

Bringing Baby Home

Before bringing the baby quaker parrot home, be sure to ask the breeder or bird store staff to check

The first day in a new home is the most common time for a baby quaker parrot to fly away.

to be sure that the bird's wing feathers are properly trimmed. The first day home is one of the most common days for an accident, when an improperly trimmed bird can fly or be blown away. Be sure that the baby bird has been trimmed in the manner suggested in this book (see pages 51–52). That is, all of the first ten feathers, the primary flight feathers, are trimmed to about a half an inch (1.3 cm) outside the covering layer of feathers.

Whether or not the new baby quaker is trimmed in this manner, we should not assume that the bird can't fly until we get to know this individual bird better. Some birds can fly with very little wing feather, and a newly purchased baby bird has no business outdoors unless it's in the cage or carrier.

A mature companion quaker can happily tolerate much cooler temperatures than most humans and many parrots, but if you have a baby quaker enduring the stress of changing homes it's a good idea to keep the baby a little warmer than usual, maybe at least 78°F (26°C) for the first week or so. If it's cold outside, warm up the car before taking the newly weaned baby to the car. Put the bird in a rigid carrier that can be belted into the car for safety.

Most dealers will give a reasonable guarantee of the bird's health. As soon as possible, take the bird to an experienced avian veterinarian for a complete blood panel and any other tests that the veterinarian recommends. Although adult quakers are sick infrequently, if illness is going to show up, it will show up in a baby.

Most states require that all parrot-type birds, especially quaker parrots, have traceable identification in order to record and document change of ownership. This means that in most states where quaker parrots may be kept legally, the baby bird will have a coded metal band around one leg. Usually, a domestically-produced baby bird will have a continuous cuff-shaped band as opposed to the old-style split, donut-shaped bands that were applied to adult birds as they passed through quarantine at the import stations. Although each band number is unique, there is no state or national registry for the band codes. For most quaker parrots, this number is the only way to document ownership.*

The band, however, can be dangerous to the bird. Be sure to ask the avian veterinarian whether or not the bird's band fits properly or should be removed. Since quakers have a frequent tendency to accidents, and broken legs resulting from caught bands are not unusual, many experienced avian veterinarians recommend removing a quaker parrot band immediately. Be sure to

Domestic band applied to baby bird (left), USDA import band applied to mature bird (right).

record the band code and save the band with the bird's health and behavior history.

If possible, go to an avian veterinarian who is unaffiliated with the

A new baby quaker parrot should be examined by an avian votorinarian as soon as possible after purchase.

---

* When a bird is DNA sexed, the owner may choose to have the DNA configuration filed with an international registry such as Zoogen, Incorporated, United States 1-800-995-BIRD, Canada 1.519.837.BIRD, Europe/UK 44.0962.880376.

There is usually only a brief time during which baby quaker parrots can be easily socialized.

dealer from whom the bird was purchased. Expect the veterinarian to recommend laboratory tests. The costs of these tests are not usually part of the bird's health guarantee from the seller, but they could save much expense and heartache down the road if the baby bird turns out to be harboring unseen illness.

If the diagnostic tests determine that the bird has a health problem, a responsible dealer honoring a guarantee will provide treatment. Some dealers will expect the bird to be returned to them for treatment.

Be careful to quarantine the new bird from contact with any other birds in the home until the veterinarian says such interaction is not dangerous. Most veterinarians will probably recommend a quarantine period of at least 30 days.

Try to bring the baby quaker home as early as possible during the day so that the bird can get its bearings before dark. Provide the baby bird with a night-light, maybe one that plugs into an electrical socket, especially if there are pets in the home that might move around in the dark.

Watch the bird carefully to determine whether or not it's eating. It is not unusual for a newly weaned baby quaker parrot to stop eating independently as a result of the stress of the move. The bird may have to be returned to the hand-feeder for a few days for reweaning, or it might be stimulated to eat by watching another bird eat. Be sure to continue the bird on the same diet it was on before coming home.

Warm foods such as oatmeal and macaroni can feel like love to a newly weaned baby quaker. Offer these warm, comfort foods daily for a while to enhance your bond with the bird as well as to guarantee a smooth transition to the new home. Eventually, the bird will probably refuse anything that seems like baby food.

Quaker parrots grow wise very quickly. They are adept at manipulating humans. We probably have a window of opportunity of no more than a month to implement appropriate socialization practices before we see unwanted behaviors begin to appear. Read the sections on behavioral development and early socialization in this book; the ability to make the most of the baby days (see the following chapter) will determine whether or not this baby bird will successfully adjust to the home.

Chapter Three
Behavioral Development

The Baby Days: Patterning for Cooperation

When a new baby quaker parrot enters the home, it is often still quaking in the manner of an infant bird. This is a window of opportunity to easily reinforce acceptable behavior and pattern the baby to an emotional baseline with the use of step-up practice.

Step-up Practice

If everyone interacting with the bird practices step ups using exactly the same verbal command, hand mannerisms, prompt location, and eye contact, and if the bird's responses have been appropriately reinforced, the bird should always respond dependably to this interaction with any person. This is a matter of people training, for allowing untrained humans to handle the bird in unfriendly, inexperienced, or provocative ways can teach the bird to bite.

With the right palm elevated, forearm perpendicular to the floor in a gesture similar to feeling for rain,

fold your thumb into your palm and rotate your palm toward your face, keeping your fingers together, until the fingertips point toward the top of the wall to the left. Your palm now faces your chin. Place the baby quaker on top of the top (index) finger. If the palm side of the index finger is the highest point on the hand, the bird's instinct to climb will keep it on the fingertip.

Since eye contact is an important part of this process, the bird must face you. If the bird is facing away from you while sitting on your hand, merely touching its tail with the other hand will usually stimulate it to turn around and face you.

With the index finger of the opposite hand (held in a mirror image of

A baby quaker parrot will be patterned to form habits that may be appropriate or inappropriate.

Approach the bird from below. The back of the front hand can actually touch the front of the back hand if you are approaching from below.

At first it may be necessary to pry the little toes up to get that first foot on the front index finger. As you lower the back hand (the hand the bird was sitting on), the bird will complete the step up onto the front (top) hand.

Practice this exercise in unfamiliar territory, out of sight of the cage, a couple of times a day for a minute or so each time. Always stop only after a successful completion of the command.

The Bite Zone

Be sure to approach the bird from below rather than in front of the feet. There is an area I call *the bite zone* that is about 1½ to 3 inches (3.8–7.6 cm) in front of the bird's feet. The bird cannot reach the hand with the feet, but can reach the hand with the beak. A sweet, well-socialized bird will gently reach out and pull the hand to the feet with the beak in order to reach the hand to step up with the foot. A poorly socialized bird might bite the hand in anger or frustration.

Gently bump the thigh where it joins the belly with the top of the index finger (with the fingerprint side up).

the hand the bird is on), gently touch the bird's thighs just below where they join the belly, maintain eye contact with the bird, and say *Step up!* clearly and distinctly. The bird should lift a foot, and place it on the finger. This method of behavioral practice involves a verbal prompt (the command) and a physical prompt (introduction of the object to be stepped on in the same place all the time).

Presenting the hand in the bite zone, then pulling it away from the bird's beak when offered (for whatever reason), is a good way to teach and reinforce biting. Once the step-up command has been given, do not move the hand away from the bird, but, rather, always move the hand toward the bird, even if encountering beaking activity. To move the hand away can seem to the bird like something running away. This activates the foremost

Once the bird has one foot on the front hand, hold it steady and drop the back hand, forcing the bird to complete the step up.

quaker behavior and the quaker motto: "If you run, I'll chase you!"

If no one ever backs down or runs away from the baby quaker parrot (allows the bird to achieve dominance by the use of aggression), the bird will not be reinforced and, therefore, will not learn to regularly attack. Do not encourage or allow anyone to wave their fingers in the bird's face or provoke the bird by poking at it with inanimate objects. Nothing could be worse for a quaker's disposition.

Transporting the Bird

The baby days are also the best time to train the bird to depend on humans for transportation from one bird-approved place to another (see Transportation Dependence, page 28). If the baby's wing feathers are kept meticulously trimmed, and if roaming is not reinforced at this time, the bird will be much easier

to keep out of trouble when the instincts for independence begin to appear.

Overbonding

It is necessary at this time to work to ensure that the bird does not become overly bonded to one

A hand presented in the "bite zone" is sure to be bit.

19

A baby parrot will become overly demanding of attention if it does not learn to play independently.

A Stimulating Environment for the Developmental Period

Some time between 6 and 18 months, the normal quaker begins showing signs of the strength of personality and independence necessary to be an adult parrot. Similar to human children in the "terrible twos," the bird will be increasingly exploratory and experimental. It might even become noisy and nippy.

If a baby quaker was well patterned to step ups and transportation dependence during the baby days and was reinforced to play alone, the "terrible twos" may be almost unnoticed, but, if these behavioral controls are not in place, the changes may be swift and shocking. This period is a tremendously important part of the young quaker parrot's behavioral development, for if the bird does not become independent, other, more troubling problems—especially shyness—may develop. Shyness and fearfulness are unusual in quaker parrots.

In the wild these juvenile birds would be busily learning survival skills. They would be following their parents and flockmates around, mimicking their activities and learning many new behaviors. I believe that opportunities to mimic, opportunities to improvise, opportunities

person to the exclusion of all others. The favorite person must enlist the aid and support of other humans to help the bird remain open and accepting of relationships with several individuals.

During the first few days in the home, it is very easy to teach the baby bird to expect constant attention by holding it too much. If the little bird does not learn to play alone, it will be overly demanding of attention and may develop related behavior problems such as screaming, biting, and feather chewing. Spend plenty of time cuddling and loving the baby, but don't cuddle all day and all night! Try not to hold a baby quaker much longer than you intend to hold it every day for the rest of its life. Be sure to reinforce playing independently, for this will be the key to *your* independence in the future.

to make successful independent decisions, and an understanding of the authority-based relationship with humans will lead a companion quaker parrot successfully through this period. Mental challenge is the key to success here.

During this period the environment must look a little like an educational nursery school. A bird that is constantly stimulated by interesting and diverse opportunities in the environment is not improvising power games and challenging human authority. We want the bird to learn to be the master of its own life, not the *all-high ruler of the universe*.

During this time a young quaker will test human patience and responses to the feel of the beak on flesh. The best way to deal with nipping at this time is to ignore the bite and the bird rather than run the risk of accidental reinforcement with drama (emotional reaction). If we simply put a biting baby bird down, it will soon learn that if it bites, it will be put down. The bird will prefer to be playing with humans, and will usually discontinue the behavior in order to be allowed to continue playing.

We might respond to persistent nipping by practicing the step-up command. If the bird is in the mood to play, and nips are rewarded with something that seems like work instead of play, then the bird will learn not to break the mood of playtime with nips. We might choose to follow the step-up practice with putting the bird down, and offering

The Wobble Correction

During the developmental period it might become necessary to respond a little more directly to test nips occurring during step-up practice. First be sure that the hand is being offered properly (coming from below and just over the feet). Then, if the bird nips the hand being offered, quickly dip the fingers of *the hand the bird is sitting on* (not the hand being offered and nipped) then return the hand to its former position.

The bird will have to stop the nip in order to regain balance. It will soon come to understand that nips during step ups cause earthquakes. This correction must be done quickly, gently, and sensitively so that the bird is not overly affected either physically or emotionally.

A well-socialized baby quaker parrot will develop extreme cooperation skills in order to be held.

Continuing Education during Adolescence

As the developmental period analogous to the "terrible twos" fades, the young quaker may become so cooperative that we are tempted to discontinue step-up practice. This is not a good idea, even if the bird seems totally docile at this time.

Usually, however, since the quaker parrot becomes sexually mature at a relatively early age, there is little separation between the developmental period and the appearance of sexually related behaviors that might be called adolescence. Unlike companion dogs and cats that are spayed and/or neutered for behavioral reasons, companion parrots must be allowed the full influence of their sexual and reproductive urges. The techniques described here are intended to enhance favorable behaviors in companion quakers and suppress or minimize most behaviors related to breeding.

Some quakers will be easily kept tame; some will be difficult. Expect every bird to be a little different, with vast differences between successfully socialized birds and unsocialized birds. The more consistent we are in all interactions, the more predictable the bird will be.

As the time to breed approaches, we see heightened exploration and physical and emotional experimentation. The bird might even change emotional and/or territorial loyalties,

an interesting toy or two. This combines work with distraction and reward.

Here again, the best response to an experimental nip is no direct reaction (especially, no overreaction), but rather planned and precise response. If nipping behavior is unintentionally rewarded with screaming, anger, or other drama, the exciting nature of the interaction might be deemed *fun* to the bird; the nipping is, therefore, rewarded. It will remain a part of the bird's behavior and will increase.

The bird will also test the limits of accepted behavior by challenging the authority of "parents" (that's you) in other ways. It is necessary to correct screaming, roaming, chasing, and any other unacceptable behaviors at this time so that they will not become a permanent part of the bird's personality.

becoming aggressive around a newly selected territory or a new favorite human (mate substitute).

If a quaker parrot has been allowed to overbond to one human in the past, at this time, the formerly favorite human might be neglected for a more easily dominated companion. We must be careful at this time to ensure that the bird is not excessively defensive of the territory around any human so that previous and predictable loyalties will not be abandoned. It might be necessary to take an arrogant young quaker parrot out of its familiar territory for at least a few days each year in order to have the opportunity to require interactions with unfamiliar humans. Vacations and indoor outings (visits to unfamiliar territory) are very helpful at this time. Even a simple car ride with the bird in a carrier can make a difference in a quaker parrot's disposition. Careful transporting in a carrier and meticulous wing feather trims will ensure safety on these outings.

Change in Control Issues

At home the adolescent quaker parrot will become increasingly concerned with control issues, especially immediate environmental control:
- The bird might start attacking tissues, or people sneezing or blowing into tissues.
- An adolescent quaker might also attack someone cleaning with quick motions with paper towels.
- An adolescent quaker might suddenly decide it loves (or hates) a

The quaker parrot may select one toy to be a surrogate enemy.

particular dog or cat or stuffed animal.
- The bird might move toys from one place to another and become increasingly agitated if someone else has the audacity to move any quaker-owned objects or return them to their previous locations. Of course, this is that nest-building instinct beginning to assert itself.

The young bird that is allowed a great deal of liberty in the home might become overly vigilant or aggressive around a suddenly and mysteriously selected territory. The adolescent quaker parrot will be seeking both companions and interlopers in its reflections so expect heightened reactions to mirrors, shiny objects, and small appliances—the bird might attack the vacuum cleaner or hair dryer. At this time the bird might fixate strongly on an inanimate object, using it either as an object of pleasure or an enemy to be attacked (see pages 24–25).

"Good Hand/Bad Hand"

The maturing parrot might begin to bite even a well-placed hand prompt for the step-up command. This might occur especially when the bird is being removed from a familiar perch, the inside, or top of the cage. Sometimes this behavior can be defeated with improved handling technique.

Maintain eye contact and offer the hand to be stepped on, approaching from below, as usual. Just as the prompt hand begins its approach to the bird, present an unfamiliar object in the bite zone (with one hand) and give the step-up command (with the other hand) followed by *Be a good bird*.

In other words, if I want a bird to step up, and it is threatening to bite the hand I want it to step on, I pick up a small object (a spoon or a TV remote or a piece of junk mail), hold it about an inch below and in front of the bird's beak, give the step-up command, and suggest good behavior. Usually the surprised bird, responding to the familiar behavioral pattern, and knowing what *Good bird* means, responds also by being what it is expected to be—a good bird.

Eye contact is especially important; a bird will often maintain eye contact rather than bite. If the bird's eye is distracted by the introduced object, it will seek to regain eye contact immediately rather than take the time to bite after being distracted.

Even if the bird bites, that unfamiliar object will be bitten rather than the hand being offered for step ups. The distraction object must be neither too large (which might frighten the bird off the perch), too small (which might be ineffective), nor toxic (soap or a piece of lead or solder).

Imagined Enemies

There must be at least one enemy who can be regularly thwarted. To a very real extent, the bird must select or identify this enemy independently, and an adolescent quaker *will do* this. Of course, it is very important for this enemy *to not be* a treasured human possession or a living creature, so several potential approved surrogate enemies must be provided. Safe, unbreakable toys such as the small-sized "Little Birdy Man" designed by Sally Blanchard or loud, safe bells are excellent candidates for this quaker-selected enemy. If an adolescent companion quaker has no opportunity to release natural aggressive parrot energy against an approved surrogate enemy at this time, the bird is likely to begin to express that natural parrot energy against whatever or whoever is closest.

If the bird is enjoying attacking a toy, leave them both alone. There will continue to be many times when the bird will solicit human attention. Those are the times when the adolescent quaker can be successfully patterned to cooperate with the use of praise, rewards, and step-up practice. The more successful behavioral experiences we have at this time, the more the bird is patterned and reinforced to cooperate, and the more likely the bird is to cooperate and when it becomes fully mature.

The Sexually Mature Companion Quaker

Aggression

There will come a time when threats might be accompanied by aggression; a bite might actually break the skin. A sexually mature companion parrot is usually more difficult to handle than a strutting little adolescent whose challenges might be mere practice for the future. At this time, new programs, people, and changes might be met with strong resistance. If, however, the bird has been patterned to accept newness and change, the bird's behavior might be maintained merely by manipulating the environment.

If a quaker parrot has not been appropriately patterned to cooperate until this time, attempts to socialize or resocialize may be met with great resistance from the bird. During this time it is not unusual for

both predictable and unpredictable bites to occur, especially in the bird's perceived "territory." Usually there will be plenty of warning: hypervigilance, eye movement, wing or tail display, or any other body language that usually accompanies aggression in this individual.

The best way to deal with aggression at this time is to give the bird space to be obnoxious. That is not to say, reinforce obnoxious behavior; never allow the quaker parrot to chase or harass. Merely return the bird to the cage in the calmest possible way. A bird nipping during a step up might be wobbled a bit on the hand it is sitting on. A bird being prompted to step up might be distracted with a toy or other inanimate object when being given the prompt for step up. I call this distraction technique "good hand/bad hand" (see page 24).

Excessive Territoriality

Lowering the bird's usual relative height, combined with increasing access to rainfall and exercise will help to minimize pent-up energy that might otherwise be expressed

The sexually mature quaker parrot might express unexpected aggression even against a best friend.

Quaker parrots are prone to forming unhealthy associations with chrome appliances.

as aggression. A bird that suddenly becomes excessively territorial must have its territory manipulated either by moving the cage or radically redesigning its interior.

Quakers are especially prone to decide that a particular chrome appliance is either a mate or a rival, leading to many courtships with toasters and wars with hair dryers. A sexually mature quaker might decide that no one is allowed near the coffeepot. A bird that has fixated on a human-owned object must be denied access to that object. A bird attacking a human-owned object might be picked up using a hand-held perch, a towel, or "good hand/bad hand," and placed with the surrogate enemy toy. Again, we must encourage and reward a companion quaker for expressing hostility against the approved enemy toy. Hostile energy will *be* expressed somehow; it is best expressed against a toy.

Excessive Vocalization

Expect to see sexual behaviors of various types. If the bird is regurgitating or masturbating on humans (see pages 76 and 77), just put it down. These activities are neither to be rewarded nor discouraged, with this exception: If the bird has a problem with excessive vocalization, reinforcement or provision for occasional sexual behaviors can sometimes replace some unnecessary vocalizing if other distraction techniques and frequent drenching showers prove ineffective.

There will continue to be many times when the bird seeks human interaction. As we will discuss in the next section, effective socialization tools such as maintenance of patterning for cooperation with step ups, transportation dependence, and an ever-changing environment remain the most dependable ways to maintain companion behavior in a mature quaker parrot.

Chapter Four
Socialization

The Behavioral Baseline

When establishing communication with another human, we know that we can successfully understand each other only if we speak the same language. Likewise, nonverbal communication must also be understood and interpreted by both parties to have the same meaning. Dog trainers establish communication with a well-socialized dog by using the *sit* command. The cues the dog receives to perform the behavior are usually both verbal and nonverbal. Similarly, practice of the step-up command establishes the lines of communication between bird and handler.

The effective handler says, *Step up* (a verbal prompt), and gives the bird something to step up on. Then:
• The well-patterned bird steps up.
• The bird is rewarded for performing the behavior.
• The bird knows what to expect.
• The handler knows what to expect.

This is an absolutely predictable interaction in which bird and handler communicate to one another that they understand each other's expectations.

The predictability of this interaction may perform an additional purpose as well. Step-up practice functions in the baby quaker's behavioral environment by providing a moment of focus, a place to begin all other activities.

This exercise is, without question, the easiest way to reinforce the authority-based relationship between humans and a tame-to-humans quaker. It is the primary mechanism by which humans establish interaction and pattern parrots to cooperate.

Practice of the step-up command establishes and maintains communication between the bird and the handler.

The quaker parrot should have one or more interesting foraging areas in which to spend time.

also have a tremendous capacity to develop cooperation skills. Transportation dependence is an extremely powerful tool for developing and maintaining cooperation skills in a tame, interactive quaker.

The concept is simple: The bird must have one or more interesting "foraging" area(s) in which to spend time. The more time the bird spends away from the cage, the less territorial behavior will be expressed at the cage. If the bird must rely on humans to provide transportation to and from the cage and play areas, it will be patterned to cooperate in order to be allowed to enjoy foraging in all possible areas.

I like to let the quaker come out of the cage to the top of the cage or door before offering the step-up prompt, and I *always* have peaceful compliance. This is the most common time for a bite, but a bite can be easily avoided with good technique and meticulous eye contact during the process of the step up from the cage.

When walking with the bird on your hand, it is sometimes helpful to cup the palm of your other hand over the bird's head and eyes to prevent the bird from jumping or falling if startled or excited. When arriving at the play area, position the bird so that the perch to be stepped on approaches the bird's thigh at approximately the same point used to prompt the step up onto the hand. I use the same command—*Step up!*—to get the bird from hand to perch as from perch to hand.

New owners of baby quakers who practice step ups twice daily outside the bird's territory benefit in several very important ways:

- The comfort of the absolutely predictable interaction can provide the human and the bird with an emotional baseline that can calm almost any emotion from fear to ferocity.
- The face-to-face activity establishes a basis for understanding the relationship hierarchy between human and bird.
- The baby quaker quickly learns to say *Step up!* when it wants to be picked up.
- The baby quaker that is well patterned to step up in unfamiliar territory is more easily patterned to cooperate at the cage.

Transportation Dependence

Some quaker parrots have a well-developed ability to abuse humans in order to maintain control. Many

Of course, the bird's compliance in this matter depends upon the regular trimming of wing feathers, for, a responsible aviculturist does not risk the loss of a quaker due to its flight ability. A flighted quaker in the home is at great danger, not only of becoming a bully, or flying out the door or window, but also of suffering serious or even fatal accidents in the home.

Balancing Human and Territorial Bonding

The Favorite Human

A quaker parrot will display a tendency to bond strongly to a single individual or territory. This bonding, in and of itself, is part of the bird's appeal, but the consequences of the bonding can instill violence in the companion bird's personality. The intensity with which the pugnacious quaker defends a bond can be formidable.

Commonly, a quaker parrot will select a particular human to be its "one-and-only" mate substitute. This human will be treated to courting and kissing, and the bird might behave totally peacefully toward this person.

However, with the appearance of sexual behaviors—regurgitation, masturbation, and egg laying—and sometimes even before, aggression may be directed toward even the favorite human. This is not at all unusual in quakers that are allowed to tolerate only one person and attack everyone else.

While being the favorite person of a tyrannical little quaker might initially seem enjoyable and even amusing, related behaviors can continue to develop in unexpected and distressing ways. It is especially unkind to both the bird and other members of the household for the favorite person to laugh when the poorly socialized quaker parrot attacks others. The laughter of the favorite human is a tremendously powerful factor in the reinforcement of behavior in any parrot, but especially so with the quaker.

Attacking the favorite human can come about as a result of either displaced aggression or the desire to dictate behavior. If an overbonded, poorly socialized little quaker is sitting on a favorite human's shoulder and a hated rival enters the room, the bird might bite, or even actually attack, the favorite person if it cannot reach the rival. Like other parrots, the quaker parrot obviously believes that, "If you're not near the one you want to bite, bite the one you're near." Displaced aggression expressed toward the favorite human is sometimes more violent than direct aggression expressed toward rivals.

In addition, a poorly socialized quaker might get the notion that it can bully its favorite person into accommodating its slightest whim, for example, Mom/Dad might be bloodied for refusing to share the

A quaker parrot that has been allowed to overbond to a particular human can switch loyalties and become overbonded to another human or a bird.

morning toast or newspaper. The more exclusive the bond, the more violent the behavior might be against all others, and ultimately, against the favorite person.

It is also quite common for birds that have been previously over-bonded to one person to switch loyalties, to overbond to a different person, and to begin attacking the previous favorite. This can be very distressing, especially if the former favorite had not been warned that this was a possibility.

These behaviors—all complications of the quaker's instinct to passionately defend bonds—are defeated with practice of step-up exercises and transportation dependence performed by anyone other than the favorite person. The bird is patterned to interact peacefully with multiple individuals by being exposed to appropriate handling by multiple individuals.

Outings

The quaker parrot's instincts to protect territory fiercely can be lessened by decreasing the amount of time spent in that territory and by allowing the bird to fulfill something resembling "exploration fantasies." As noted earlier, simulated vacations and indoor outings into unfamiliar territory are especially effective in reducing territorial aggression in the companion quaker parrot; however, careful transportation and meticulous wing feather trims must be maintained to ensure the quaker parrot's safe return from these outings.

It is particularly beneficial for a quaker parrot to take outings into unfamiliar territory with less-than-favorite humans. This behavior technique works by improving the bond between the parrot and that human. If the bird is out in public, perhaps at the office, the bank, or the mall, and there is only one familiar human around, if that human is handling the bird appropriately and compassionately, then that human will immediately become the favorite human in that scary place. This is an "emotional rescue."

This change of heart may be only temporary and may be lost upon returning home. Once again, behavior isn't linear; the improved behavior may come and go and will become habitual only if it is repeated. Commonly, the person who takes the time to include a quaker parrot on outings will be treated very well, both out of the home territory and back in the home territory. That person may still be limited in terms of access and interaction at the quaker's cage but will enjoy the bird's good disposition at all other locales, such as stationary and portable perches, etc.

If the quaker parrot is well patterned to step up to a hand-held perch, even the less-than-favorite human should be able to remove the bird easily from the cage with a perch. This gives no opportunity to accidentally pattern biting at the cage. The bird can be taken to another location outside its fiercely protected territory, where all can enjoy a full range of quaker affection and cooperation behaviors.

Outings with the least favored person in the house are a tremendously powerful way to defeat over-bonding to one person. Even a visit to the veterinarian or groomer is often automatically beneficial in the generation of cooperative, docile behaviors and more balanced attitudes toward all humans in the home. Actually, this is an extension of the rescue scenario. If outings can be combined with some sort of rescue—maybe "saving" the bird from the groomer, it will have even more lasting effect.

If the bird is returned to the same behavioral environment as before, the behavior will regress and the new pattern of trust will be lost. The behavioral effects of an outing must be reinforced by improved handling techniques by the less-favored persons lest those new behaviors return to what they were before.

Change Is Good

Any type of parrot can become excessively concerned with control

Quaker parrots should be frequently patterned to interact outside their home territory.

The Rescue Scenario

In the fable of Androcles and the lion, a lion refuses to attack a slave who previously had removed a thorn from its paw. Likewise, a quaker that is rescued from physical or emotional pain may learn to favor even a hated rival. Opportunities to "rescue" a companion quaker may come at any time, but the most common and predictable opportunities include the groomer and the veterinarian.

The bird's favorite person puts the bird into its carrier, and the bird is transported to the groomer or veterinarian by the less-favored human. After the bird has been poked, prodded, filed, and trimmed, the less-favored human will, by comparison, seem much nicer than the awful groomer or veterinarian. A few cuddles, step-ups, "pretty birds" and "poor babies" can soften even the fiercest quaker's attitude to a less-favored human.

The quaker parrot's cage and play areas should be frequently rearranged.

of its cage territory, but quakers are exceptionally likely to do so. If a parrot's cage is left for years in the same location, if perches and toys are not occasionally rearranged, we risk the danger of the bird developing the assumption that it can *completely control* its environment. Resulting aggression should not be surprising.

Quaker parrots are especially receptive to manipulation of environmental elements as a means of controlling aggression. We can reduce aggression in and around the cage, by moving it at least a couple of times each year. This could mean merely reversing the position of the cage and the areas to which the bird is transported for play (foraging) time.

Weekly introduction of new or rotated elements into the cage environment can greatly lessen the quaker parrot's instinct for control. The more often the quaker parrot's cage is rearranged, the

less likely the bird is to exhibit aggression in and around the cage and the more likely the bird will remain tame.

The quaker parrot's ability to tolerate change can be seen in the wild bird's ability to adjust to impermanence in nature when large and small colony nests are sometimes destroyed in storms or other predictable disasters.

Nesting quaker parrots are constantly assembling, disassembling, and reassembling their huge communal nests. It's not unusual for one family's babies to come tumbling out onto the ground if a neighbor removes just one wrong stick at the wrong time.* If a companion quaker parrot is not provided with a variety of interesting, reasonable changes, we will begin to see ill effects on its behavior by the time the bird is one year old.

Some quaker parrots are intolerant of human intervention in the arrangement of toys. We can mitigate this aggression by rearranging perches and toys frequently, and by rearranging them when the bird is out of sight of the cage.

Failure to rearrange and rotate environmental elements can sometimes have adverse effects on a quaker parrot's behavioral development. A quaker parrot that is conditioned to accept change at an early age is also less likely to develop fearful behaviors and inappropriate

---

* Ilse Goshorn, quaker parrot breeder, interview, 1989.

responses to stress, both conditions that can lead to feather problems as the bird matures.

Environmental Enrichment

The quaker parrot's ancestors evolved a metabolism that was well equipped to cope with a life of wild independence. The companion quaker's indoor environment is often missing important elements such as flying, foraging, assembling, and recovering from being wet that the bird would be experiencing in the wild. These activities enable the bird to express energy. When energy is unused, as in a wing feather-trimmed bird (read here "couch potato") sitting in a cage, that energy is frequently expressed as inappropriate behavior.

In the wild the bird would be physically and intellectually stimulated by elements of the environment, especially those elements related to survival. The wild quaker spends most of its time foraging for food. In captivity we provide the food in a bowl. We must find ways for the bird to use the energy it would use during foraging in the wild. For quaker parrots, that means teaching the bird, at an early age, to play alone; toys are the tools to achieve this end, but almost anything can be a toy.

I was stunned when I returned home one day, to find that Tza-tza, my three-year-old quaker, had

somehow managed to escape and had spent his time removing tissues from a pop-up box and hauling them into his cage. Now, when I see a feather-chewing quaker, I often wonder what would happen if the owners merely gave the bird a fresh box of tissue to decimate every few days.

Since the quaker parrot is a nest builder, many birds benefit from opportunities to gather and assemble nesting materials. Flexible twigs and coffee stirrers might be woven into elaborate ersatz nests, and a quaker parrot that is building is not screaming or chasing.

All parrots spend more time foraging for food than any other activity. Part of foraging involves flying around; obviously a wing feather-trimmed bird is not going to be doing that! We can replace some of the lost enterprise (opportunities to express energy)—burn off the calories and frustration that need to be burned off—by treating the bird to frequent drenching showers. Although the

Access to appropriate stimuli provides quaker parrots with opportunities to improve mental and physical prowess.

quaker's native range is often made up of areas of low rainfall, and the bird has little need for the extra moisture, in captivity frequent drenching showers can replace flying as the primary means of using excess energy. The energy expressed by bathing and recovering from being wet will help to prevent some of those temper tantrums the quaker can have so frequently in captivity.

Another part of foraging involves decision-making processes. I believe all parrots will have more stable emotions and more confident dispositions from having access to appropriate choices. For instance, I like to introduce more than one element, such as toys and/or perches, at a time. Since every toy and every perch I provide is appropriate, no matter which one the bird chooses, the decision will be perceived by all to be a successful decision and the bird will have a happy, potentially self-rewarding interaction with its environment. Even if the bird does not choose to play with a particular toy or to spend time on a particular perch, its presence provides the bird with opportunities to feel happy and confident as a result of making a successful decision between the alternatives.

A quaker parrot with no understanding of time might feel abandoned and overpreen or chew off feathers when humans go on vacation.

An Understanding of Time

Also missing from life outdoors is instant access to an understanding of what time of day it is. In nature certain things happen at the same time every day: The sun comes up, travels across the sky, goes down; shadows are long, then short, then disappear, then are long again. Certain creatures come and go at the same time every day: Nocturnal creatures go to sleep soon after sunrise; fireflies come out just before dark; everybody naps at midday.

In many living rooms, a bird can see little of the passing of time. A companion parrot might see the progression of the sun across the sky, but probably, in most homes, they see only that there is light at the window sometimes and darkness at the window other times.

The intelligent companion quaker develops confidence and independence from understanding time. This is especially helpful in the prevention of abandonment-related behavioral disorders such as screaming and feather picking.

Sometimes, something as simple as telling a bird, *I'll be right back!* before leaving the room can prevent attention-demanding vocalizations. If the human keeps the promise to return quickly, the human-bonded companion quaker will learn very quickly what these words mean. I know a conure that says, *I'll be right back* when it walks out of the room, and if a conure can say it with understanding, a quaker can say it with understanding.

Time Markers

In order to teach the bird what constitutes a day, a "time marker" can be provided by arranging to have the television come on and go off at the same time every day. Ideally, a mid-afternoon game show or children's program with lots of color and excitement will more likely hold a bird's interest. Even if the bird doesn't choose to watch the television program, it will notice the theme song, and know that it is mid-afternoon and that the "flock" will be home for dinner soon.

Humans have the opportunity to explain to the bird that some things happen *before* "TV Time" and some things happen *after* "TV Time." Every day when we leave, we say to the bird, *I'll be back after TV Time.*

When preparing to vacation away from a young quaker parrot for the first time, we are more likely to come home to a bird with feathers and a happy disposition if we explain to the bird exactly how long we will be gone. (Actually, it's not unusual for a quaker parrot to welcome a favorite human home from vacation with one punishing bite!)

To condition a quaker parrot to tolerate a longer vacation, begin by explaining to the bird that *We'll be back after one TV Time. We'll be back after two TV Times; that means we'll be back in two days.*

Chris Davis, one of the first to work in the field of companion bird behavior modification, suggests that we count out the number of days we will be away from home by showing the number with fingers laid across the palm of the other hand.

Counting

It's important to teach the quaker parrot to understand numbers by counting as we drop favored pieces of foods into its bowl. I know that these birds can understand numbers but I'd love to hear that someone has *scientifically* demonstrated that their quaker can count. We have learned from Dr. Irene Pepperberg's work with Alex, the African gray parrot, that an African gray can answer questions about shapes, colors, and numbers of familiar objects. I believe that Dr. Pepperberg's studies with Alex could be duplicated or at least approximated with quaker parrots.

If the bird understands that *one TV Time* equals one day, then it will learn to understand what it means when we say that we will be back after *two TV Times.* If we gradually increase the number of days we are away, the bonded companion quaker is much less likely to suffer adverse behavioral reactions than if we simply leave for a two- or three-week vacation without letting the bird know what to expect.

Establishing time markers in the environment is also helpful in conditioning a quaker parrot to tolerate being "abandoned" during the day. That is, if the bird is accustomed to having an in-home companion all day, and that companion decides to go to work outside the home, the bird may develop adverse behavioral reactions. If TV Time is well established before any radical schedule changes are made, the bird will not usually react negatively to other changes; TV Time will be a constant in an ever-changing world. The presence of constants like this helps the bird to tolerate those changes.

Cuckoo clocks or other instruments that sound the hour are also beneficial. Don't introduce them immediately into the room with the bird, however, as such an instrument can sometimes seem like an intruder. It is better to put it in the next room either permanently or temporarily.

It's not unusual to hear stories about the quaker parrot's understanding of time or the passage of time. I often come across reports about quaker parrots that seem to be able to either "read" clocks or have some other means of knowing what time it is. Quaker parrots often become quiet and withdrawn just before favored humans leave or enthusiastic and vocal minutes just before they return.

Acquiring Human Speech

Just as a baby quaker can be virtually *guaranteed* to be occasionally nippy, a baby quaker that was sensitively hand-fed and socialized by talking humans can be virtually *guaranteed* to talk. These gifted little mimics learn what they hear, so if the hand-feeders talk to the baby birds, the baby birds learn to use the hand-feeders' words to attract attention in order to be fed.

Since most elements of the quaker's language are learned, if you wish a quiet bird, seek a baby that was not raised around noisy imported or breeding groups of quakers. If talking is important, ask the hand-feeder which babies are already talking, for many baby quakers will acquire a few human words before they are weaned. In this respect a quaker parrot probably provides more immediate gratification than an African gray. I believe a quaker can develop just as many words as a gray parrot, but with less mimicking accuracy and understandability than the African gray.

It is not necessary to drive the bird crazy with recordings or redundant sessions in the corner or in the dark, for a baby quaker will learn to say what it hears spoken often and with enthusiasm. Talk to other humans and pets in the way you expect the quaker to talk to you: *Hi! What cha doin'? Gimme a kiss* are easy places to start. It is almost impossible for the hand-fed baby quaker, socialized in the manner suggested in this book, not to learn to say *Step up!* with some understanding of its meaning.

It is especially recommended that you talk to the bird while it is inside the cage. This is manipulation of barrier frustration, the bird's desire to be outside the cage. It's very easy to stimulate a quaker parrot to talk to achieve its desire to get out of the cage. It's possible even to teach a quaker parrot to use appropriate words to ask (or demand) to be let out.

Teaching phrases and groups of words that involve ritualized answers or responses are beneficial in generating other behaviors, even other talking behaviors, as demonstrated in the following story:

My own quaker parrot, Tza-tza thinks that my coughing fits due to asthma, involve ritualized response. When I cough, he coughs along with me. When I stop coughing, he says, in the most precious voice you can imagine, *Are you OK?*

While quaker parrots are well known for using words with an understanding of their meaning, they have a tendency to assign their own meanings to certain words. For example, Tza-tza has heard me scold my yellow-naped Amazon, Portia, many times for unwanted vocalizations at inappropriate times. Tza-tza thinks that the word *Portia!!!* spoken in a firm, scolding way means, *Be quiet, you noisy Amazon!*

So, whenever any of the Amazons at my house scream—Saucey,

Lolita, Portia, or Penelope—Tza-tza says, *Portia!!!* meaning, *Be quiet, you noisy Amazon!*

Baby quaker parrots often acquire human speech while they are still being hand-fed.

The Power of Positive Reinforcement

Once, long ago, a tall, shy man brought his baby cockatiel to me for "taming." The bird was a precious, parent-raised cinnamon pearl hen. The owner was unsuccessfully trying to teach her to enjoy human touch. She would not step up or allow petting. Seeking to scratch the little bird's neck, the tall man would quietly, stiffly reach out to her, and she would threaten to bite him. It was a behavior that he couldn't ignore.

I said, "Talk to her the way you talk to your wife. Tell her that she's pretty, and that you love her, and want her to be happy."

The man gave me a strange look, then practiced whispering sweet words to the little bird who seemed to just melt in his hands, learning in somewhat less than half an hour not only to step up, but also to allow petting.

A few weeks later, bird and owner returned for a grooming lesson. The little cockatiel was sweet, tame, and affectionate. When I commented on the changes—the well-reinforced step-up response, etc.—the happy cockatiel owner grinned and said, "If you think that's something, you should see the change in my wife!"

This wise young man had learned that *verbal reinforcement* (praise) in anticipation of good behavior (cooperation) is one of the strongest tools available in the modification of any kind of creature's behavior. He had applied this technique to socialize his cockatiel. He had also successfully applied this technique to improve a human relationship.

Accidental Reinforcement

While certain spouses and baby cockatiels obviously respond well to loving praise, even the wickedest,

Sweet, loving verbal "caresses" can induce a quaker parrot to enjoy petting.

Kiwi, the Quaker that Sets Things Straight

Kiwi, my little green quaker, has an extensive vocabulary. The only problem was that he only spoke around family members. When company was over, he zipped his beak, only to make me look like a lying fool. But this behavior was about to be solved by accident one day by a friend of mine. She came over for a visit, and we were trying to coax Kiwi into saying, "I'm a cute little leprechaun," one of his favorite sayings.

My friend said it the wrong way. She said, "I'm a *pretty* little leprechaun."

All of a sudden, Kiwi perked up, cocked his head, and, eyeing her suspiciously, said, "I'm a cute little leprechaun!"

He just couldn't tolerate her ignorance!

Now all you have to do to get Mr. Tweezerbird to talk is to have company say things the wrong way.

Paulette Jacob
Covington, Louisiana

wildest quaker can respond to conscientious application of positive reinforcement. Actually, it's quite common to accidentally reinforce behavior, especially in a creature that is looking for any kind of attention. A normal, creative quaker parrot that is trained to anticipate rewards for good behavior also usually becomes more willing to seek

Harvesting Behavior

I have yet to see a description of wild quaker parrot behavior that did not mention what can be identified as gathering or harvesting behavior. The quaker parrot is often observed to take one or two bites from a whole fruit, then drop the fruit to the ground. This behavior, which is also reported in wild cockatoos, is said to turn perfectly reasonable farmers murderous.

Once, when I was studying a pair of feral quakers here in Denver, Colorado, I came to understand the purpose of this behavior. The birds were raiding a backyard corn patch every morning at 11 A.M. We could watch them easily from inside the house. The homeowners felt very blessed to be visited by parrots in this unusual locale, and wished to protect the birds.

At traditional harvest time the birds were observed to drop much more corn on the ground than they would eat. We were puzzled by this behavior, although, as I said before, it is often reported from the bird's native range. As the winter progressed, we could see the purpose and value of this practice, for no matter how cold it was or how much snow was on the ground, those two birds knew exactly where to find that corn. The homeowners reported that they once watched the birds dig through 5 inches (13 cm) of snow to reach the cache of corn.

new ways to generate rewards and will gradually abandon activities that are not occasionally reinforced.

Laughter is probably the most powerful reinforcement for a companion quaker. Screaming or drama of any kind can also reinforce behavior; therefore, if a human receiving a painful bite overreacts—screams, jumps, runs, cusses—a quaker parrot might continue or repeat the behavior for the "fun" of the interaction.

Verbal Reinforcement

Using verbal reinforcement may sound subtle, but the results can be dazzling. The quaker parrot is an extremely verbal animal. Verbal reinforcement is absolutely the easiest way for most people to perpetuate desirable behavior in these little parrots. Praise as reinforcement is often used successfully, even though humans may be unaware that they are reinforcing behavior in this way. A verbal praise style of training might be more commonly used naturally or as a matter of conditioning by females, which might be the reason that a large number of companion quakers appear to favor females.

Other Rewards

Although food is extremely important to some birds, some quakers don't appear to be influenced by food rewards at all. Also, their ability to be easily reinforced by food

Rewards of both food and affection can work effectively to reinforce desirable behavior.

widely accepted, is sometimes eclipsed by rewards of affection in the training of hand-fed domestic parrots. In fact, emotional rewards may be more effective than food rewards when reinforcing behavior in most hand-fed quaker parrots. It might be beneficial, however, to try food rewards when rehabilitating a recaptured bird, a neglected handfed gone wild, or a particular bird resisting other types of reinforcement.

Some stubborn individual quakers might have to be half-starved before they will take food from the human hand and eat it. Additionally, because of their tendency to harvest, effective food rewards must be given in very, very small pieces. If food rewards are given in larger than quaker-bite-sized pieces, the bird becomes more and more fixated on grabbing and hoarding chunks of food, and other behaviors become impossible to generate. For the purpose of generating and maintaining appropriate behavior, it's usually easier to reward a hand-fed companion quaker with laughter, kisses, cuddles, and a generous environment *before* undesirable behaviors appear.

rewards may be mitigated by their gathering behaviors. Some individuals might take reward after reward only to drop one after another on the ground. This is not usually agitation, distraction, or stress response as seen in some other parrots. Few of these quaker parrots are demonstrating alienation; they may be exhibiting normal gathering behaviors, or, like cockatoos, many hand-fed quakers might be simply so crazy about people that they would rather play or cuddle than eat whenever humans are near.

Traditional, old-time parrot training depended almost entirely on food rewards. This technique, though still

The Setup

The first step to molding a quaker's behavior with verbal rewards is to teach the meaning of the words *Good bird.* Most quaker parrots respond emotionally to melodious voices in soothing tones. Teaching a bird the meaning of *Good bird* usually comes very naturally, as a cooing intonation of the word conveys the meaning quite effectively. The bird may stretch, puff out, and wag its tail in response to a successfully awarded verbal caress. When we can see that the bird knows what *Good bird* means, then the *Good bird* verbal reward can be used to reinforce any appropriate behavior. We can also reward the bird any time it is not engaging in inappropriate behavior. The words *Good bird* can even, under some circumstances, be used to suggest— and, therefore, to guide—good behavior in a bird that is misbehaving or about to misbehave.

Be careful not to overdo verbal praise; too much adoration can seem like a courtship to a sex-starved little quaker. If strutting, neck stretching, feather-flaring sexual displays are frequently reinforced, we might wind up with a beautiful little fire-breathing dragon that bites, chases, masturbates, and decorates the cage with regurgitated food.

Anticipation

In recent years, I've come to believe that it is usually undesirable to use negative terms such as *Bad bird,* especially when we are prompting the bird to step up. If we want a quaker parrot to do something, we must be giving only one message at a time. It's very confusing to hear both *Step-up* and *No* or *Don't bite* at the same time. I now prefer to use the words *Good bird* to both reinforce appropriate

Quaker parrots are observed to "harvest" food by dropping it to the ground and returning for it later.

behavior and to prevent inappropriate behavior.

As with other parrots, positive reinforcement of appropriate behavior, not punishment for inappropriate behavior, is the most effective means of ensuring long-term cooperation from a quaker parrot. Yelling *No, Don't,* or *Stop* will interrupt a behavior only momentarily. The bird will stop, look up, then go back to the previous (inappropriate) behavior.

Telling that quaker, *Be a good bird!* not only stops the inappropriate behavior; it suggests to the bird the appropriate behavior that should follow.

The bird learns that fulfilling the command, *Be a good bird!* brings all sorts of happy rewards.

A sensitive handler can see a bite coming, but no amount of yelling *Bad bird* will stop a quaker from biting when given the opportunity. On the other hand, a calm, authoritative demeanor combined with eye contact and a stern verbal reprimand, *You'd better be a good bird!*

reminds the bird that you are the boss, and that good things come to good birds. You will have stimulated appropriate behavior by reminding the bird of your expectations and the rewards that go with them. You will have also reinforced a desirable pattern that is then more likely to remain habitual. It may sometimes be necessary to combine this technique with a Wobble Correction (see page 21).

Softly and sweetly reminding a quaker parrot to *Be a good bird* is especially persuasive during practice of step-up exercises and when used in combination with "Good Hand/Bad Hand" (see page 24). This suggests to the bird what to do next—to be good and/or pretty. These words can often generate appropriate self-rewarding activities in a well-socialized quaker parrot. The bird will discontinue what it is doing and initiate playing, talking, or preening behaviors.

When delivered sharply, firmly, and with authority, the words *Be a good bird!* can stop a well-socialized quaker in its tracks. This might be used in combination with a hand clap or slapping a newspaper or magazine against the table if the bird is attacking or chasing and we are too far away to intervene physically. Again, we have both stopped the unwanted behavior and suggested appropriate—often self-rewarding—behavior to follow.

Maintaining Status in the Pecking Order

Quaker parrots commonly abuse humans who appear (to the bird) to be of lower status in the flock. This is related to wild behavior in which sick birds are attacked and driven away so that they won't attract predators to the flock. If the bird doesn't see a particular human as dominant, that human is likely to be perceived as having lower status and might then be treated as territory, a possession, an intruder, or a rival.

A successful relationship between human and companion bird casts the human in the role of loving parent. Because parrots have a strong instinct to understand what is expected of them, a loving, authority-based relationship is probably the best way to maintain a long-term relationship between human and parrot. This is easily accomplished with the frequent (most days) practice of the step-up command, which patterns the bird to cooperate with other human expectations.

It is difficult to maintain a long-term, peaceful relationship with a quaker parrot that is allowed to choose access to the human shoulder; this is doubly true for a poorly patterned bird. It is almost impossible to give a step-up command and maintain eye contact with a quaker parrot on one's shoulder. Additionally, if the bird gets the notion that it has a right to the "dominant position" on a human shoulder, then that human might wind up being treated as territory or a possession. An angry quaker parrot expressing overt or displaced aggression when sitting on a human shoulder can do painful damage to sensitive eye, ear, nose, and lip tissue, especially on children.

Extraneous body language—waving hands about and bobbing heads—can seem to indicate insecurity on the part of the human and can be very provocative to a nippy bird. Just as parrots that favor females may be responding to a particular style of reinforcement, parrots that favor males may be expressing an attraction to stolid body language and comfortable use of authority. The bird's behavior can be changed by coaching the human client either to improve nurturing or effective authority interactions.

While one bird responds to snuggling and praise, another bird might respond to authority. In most cases, however, both behavioral tools must

It is difficult to maintain a long-term, peaceful relationship with a quaker parrot that is allowed to choose access to the human shoulder.

be in place and balanced for the quaker to maintain acceptable companion behavior throughout its long life. Without loving reinforcement, the use of authority is inappropriate and usually ineffective. Without authority, the loving reinforcement might not be enough.

Potty Training

While a quaker parrot's droppings are neither large nor foul smelling, many people prefer to train a companion bird to avoid soiling human clothing or furnishings with droppings. This can be accomplished by socializing the bird to void on an approved surface or location. The bird is thus patterned to defecate on the cage, perch, or a newspaper.

Potty training works exactly like any other kind of parrot training: We generate the desired behavior, then reinforce it until it becomes habitual.

In this case, that doesn't usually take long.

To generate the behavior, we must understand it. A quaker parrot probably defecates about every 20 to 40 minutes, more often if it's nervous. It will usually defecate every time it changes locations. For example, we can expect a bird to defecate every time we move it from cage to perch or perch to cage.

Humans can calculate the time between droppings, then anticipate the behavior by picking up the bird before it defecates. Hold the bird over a newspaper and praise or pet it as reinforcement when the behavior occurs.

It is particularly helpful to play with the bird during the first part of the cycle—just after the bird defecates—then put the bird down to play alone for about ten minutes, before picking it up again to facilitate the enactment and reinforcement of the behavior.

It's best to avoid training a quaker parrot to potty on a verbal command. The quaker parrot is a spontaneous and self-motivated creature. Although I cannot document a quaker parrot dying from waiting for the human command to defecate, I can document that tragedy in another New World species, the macaw. It's not worth risking a quaker parrot's health for the fun of showing people that the bird will defecate on a verbal command.

In some companion quakers, because of their desire for human handling, potty-trained behavior appears spontaneously. If the bird figures out that it is put down when it poops on people, and if it wants to be held, it will discontinue pooping on people in order to continue to be held.

Chapter Five

General Care

The Cage

Size

A quaker parrot that spends adequate time outside the cage in appropriate play areas can do very well in a modest-size cage. If the bird does little more than sleep in the cage, I think a quaker parrot can be happy in as little as four cubic feet (1.3 cu m) of space in the roost cage.

I must emphasize that this is a *minimum* cage, and one that would be adequate if the bird slept in the cage and spent no more than three or four waking hours in the cage. This presupposes that the bird has frequent access to additional play areas (see the sections on Foraging Territory, pages 48–49, and Transportation Dependence, pages 28–29).

At the same time, an excessively large cage can contribute to behavior problems if the bird learns to avoid cooperating to come out of the cage. It is seldom difficult to entice a quaker to leave a small cage—simply open the door. If the cage is small, the quaker parrot is probably best patterned to step up off the door or cage top. In an appropriately sized training cage, if the bird chooses not to come out, it can be easily convinced to "choose" to come out by removing the bottom grill and tray and turning the cage upside down, setting it on its top. The bird will readily step up off the "top" of the upside down cage, even if it will not usually step up willingly and peacefully from the actual top of the cage.

It can be quite difficult to convince a territorial quaker parrot to leave a very large cage. If the cage is a flight or walk-in cage, the bird must be especially well patterned to step up to the human hand from inside the cage. If the bird is nippy, patterning to step up on a hand-held perch might be necessary in a flight or walk-in cage.

Although the quaker parrot chews a good deal less than the other (cavity breeding) parrots, they can easily chew through most wooden or bamboo cages. Because of the quaker parrot's suspected sensitivity to zinc, avoid cages made with any type of galvanized or zinc-soldered material. The safest metal finishes for a quaker's cage appear to be brass or stainless steel. Even those beautiful, usually expensive, "powder coated" finishes are high in zinc and might contribute to feather

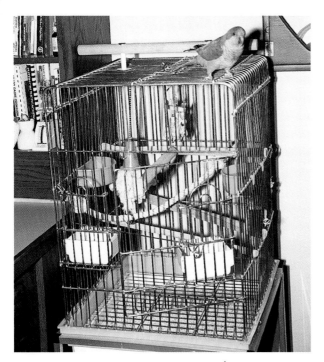

This cage is appropriately sized to prevent behavior problems that can develop in a cage that is too large.

chewing in companion quaker parrots (see Feather Problems, pages 72–73).

Avoid cages with wide spacing between the wires, lest a curious quaker get its head caught. Bars should be less than 1 inch (2.5 cm) apart. Quakers have less tendency to climb than many other types of parrots such as Amazons, so they can tolerate a glass enclosure so long as many interesting branches and climbing and playing opportunities are provided. I prefer a flat-topped cage for the play area provided by the top. Quaker parrots also tolerate a grill on the bottom of the cage, although many of them will learn to pull paper and trash up through the grill for entertainment.

Perches

Be sure to provide perches that are small enough for quaker parrot feet. Both hand-held and stationary perches should be furnished in a variety of easy-to-grip sizes. A bird cannot grip a perch unless the opposing toes extend at least a little more than halfway around the branch. Especially if the bird falls frequently, soft-wood branches such as ailanthus, sumac, or any of the poplar family are preferable to hardwood perches like manzanita, which is more suitable for full-sized macaws and cockatoos.

Covers

A fairly opaque—but not light-proof—cover will facilitate sleeping and noise control; a lightproof cover would neutralize the benefits of the night light we use to prevent injuries caused by darkness. A quaker parrot sleeping in complete darkness might thrash about in fear and be hurt if it perceives movement in the room.

Temperature

A healthy quaker parrot can tolerate much cooler temperatures than most humans can. There is actually evidence to suggest that the quaker parrot's immune system might be stronger as a result of some exposure to a cooler environment. A companion quaker living indoors can easily tolerate temperatures down to 40°F (4.4°C), assuming there are no drafts.

Height

The height of the cage is tremendously significant in the development and prevention of aggression. A quaker parrot housed higher than everyone in the house, especially children, might decide that it is the household "avenging angel" and will learn to punish everyone that comes into its territory. It is better to situate the cage no higher than chest height of the shortest family member.

Location

Even the location of the cage is important. Place the quaker parrot's cage well away from traffic areas where people move quickly; a person rushing past the quaker's territory can stimulate the chasing behaviors and territorial aggression that are so well developed in the quaker parrot.

It is especially important to place the cage well away from a doorway that people often rush through. If the bird is next to the doorway and doesn't hear someone coming, it can seem to the bird that that person appeared out of thin air, which can lead to all kinds of unfortunate behavior from biting to feather picking. If, in spite of the best possible choice of location in a particular room, the bird is startled whenever you rush through the door, let it know that you are coming by whistling or speaking before you appear.

Cleaning the Cage

Since quaker parrots are not cavity breeders, they chew less, and, therefore, make a little less mess than other parrots, but they're still

A flat-topped cage provides a play area on the top.

birds—and birds are messy. The easier a cage is to clean, the less likely that the bird will be homeless some day. Ease in cleaning may even be the most significant factor in whether or not the bird succeeds in its first home. The mess-catcher feature (horizontal extensions that catch debris before it reaches the floor) is optional (and sometimes expensive) with some cages. It is usually worth the extra cost.

I once heard Dr. Susan Clubb lecture on the suitability of various substrata (materials for the bottom of the cage and play perch). She reported that laboratory studies demonstrated that, in terms of disease prevention, newspaper with ink was superior to all other substances studied because it seems that the ink retards the growth of bacteria and other dangerous microorganisms.

Dishes

If the cage comes with only two dishes, be sure to purchase at least one additional dish so that dry foods, wet foods, and water can be provided in separate dishes. Actually, keeping the bowls clean is much easier if you have two complete sets for each cage. I just replace the dishes and run the other set through the dishwasher every day. A quaker parrot is not the easiest creature in the world to live with. If cleaning the bird's cage is a difficult chore, humans may feel resentment, which can easily affect their relationship with the bird. Be easy on yourself and buy the most well-designed cage possible.

Foraging Territory

Separate play areas are necessary to prevent boredom, lessen territorial aggression at the cage, balance bonding, and facilitate cooperation skills through transportation dependence. I like having

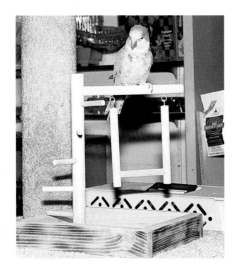

Table-top play perches are inexpensive and easy to find in appropriate sizes for quakers.

at least one portable and one fixed, freestanding play area.

While tabletop play perches are inexpensive, easy to find, and often of appropriate size, a quaker parrot on a portable perch can get into a great deal of trouble if it can easily hop off the perch to the coffee table or countertop. Roaming can be fatal. We can sometimes defeat this behavior by placing the portable perch on a backless bar stool. If the base of the portable perch is larger than the seat of the stool, then the wing feather-trimmed and appropriately socialized bird will be restricted to the perch.

I also like having at least one freestanding floor perch, preferably one with a mess catcher. I love the perches that look like giant Tinker Toys. I am, however, still just enough of a traditionalist to be very fond of freestanding softwood "trees." The weed trees—sumac and ailanthus—are excellent used in this way for quaker parrots. Clean and disinfect branches with bleach water, being sure to rinse and dry thoroughly. Then mount chest-high forked ailanthus branches or whole sumac trees in Christmas tree stands, add toys and dishes, and watch the fun. If the first fork of the tree branches off at least 30 inches (76 cm) from the floor, the bird cannot get down easily. If the highest branch is no higher than the shortest family member's chin, the bird will be less likely to develop aggression on the perch. Some very short family members must be provided with a step stool, perhaps the type that has two steps and a handle.

Always keep appropriately sized handheld perches available nearby and pattern the bird to step ups on handheld perches so that even the smallest or least favored family member can handle the bird when it is in a cranky mood. Behavior becomes habit by repetition. If the bird bites someone more than once, that behavior is easier to repeat and is in danger of becoming habitual. It is better to handle the bird with handheld perches than to give the bird the opportunity to develop a pattern of damaging human skin. A bird that damages human skin is also damaging human confidence, and this can do irreversible damage to the relationship between that human and that bird.

Toys and Playing

A quaker parrot that does not learn to play alone is at risk of being neglected later in life. In other words, if the bird demands constant human attention, it is in danger of being physically and emotionally abandoned. A physically and emotionally abandoned bird is an abused bird; it will develop behavior problems as a response to that abuse.

Odd behavior can develop when the baby quaker has too little to do: It might bite or scream because it has unused energy, or it might begin excessive grooming, such as preen-

A toy for a quaker parrot must be small enough to be easily held and manipulated by the bird.

ing feathers until they are damaged, chewing or filing nails, or sharpening the upper mandible on the cage or perch.

If we fill the bird's waking hours with step ups, outings, climbing, flapping, playing, and bathing, the bird is less likely to develop unwanted behaviors. Playing is especially important and usually comes naturally to the quaker parrot, although each quaker will learn different behaviors from its family flock. This animal is a parrot, which means it mimics—as best it can—the behavior of its companions. It's not unusual for humans in homes where a bird does not play to admit that humans in the home do not play either.

Playing is self-rewarding behavior, and truly self-rewarding behavior requires no outside reinforcement to be perpetuated. If the bird enjoys several interesting, self-rewarding behaviors, it will never develop behavior problems unless it is mishandled by poor socialization in interactions directly with human hands.

A plastic self-locking cable tie is a safe substitute for almost any kind of toy fastener. The cable tie should be pulled completely closed rather than left open, which may represent a toe hazard.

Playing can also be used to distract a bird from undesirable behavior such as screaming. If the bird can be induced to play with a toy rather than make obnoxious noises, then *the bird* can administer its own rewards, and the distracted behavior is easier to perpetuate.

A small, bird-safe bell is an ideal toy to serve as both a best friend and a surrogate enemy.

A quaker parrot won't destroy hardwood toys the way a cavity-breeding parrot would. Hard plastic and metal toys are relatively indestructible. A quaker will remove the toys from the cage and will sometimes dismantle them, but won't turn them into toothpicks as a cockatoo will. Quaker parrots will destroy rope and leather toys.

Look for safe toys from reputable companies that use guaranteed bird-safe fasteners and welded chain. While we have long known to avoid jingle bells (with the dangerous slits that can trap and cut little toes) and split rings (like those used for keys) for their dangerous potential, Dianalee Deter of Paradise Found, a Colorado bird store, reports that her quaker recently found a new potentially dangerous item. Dianalee says that she had always been careful to provide only (presumably safe) quick-link-type fasteners for toys. One day she found her quaker parrot hanging from the top of her cage with a small, open, quicklink penetrating the skin inside the cavity under her beak. Now Dianalee replaces all quicklinks with larger, fatter quicklinks at least an inch-and-a-half (3.8 cm) long.

Another compelling report from one of the world's foremost avian veterinarians provides an entirely different reason for avoiding quicklinks altogether. Greg J. Harrison, DVM, who literally wrote "the book" on avian medicine (*Avian Medicine, Principles and Application,* Ritchie, Harrison & Harrison, Wingers Publishing, Inc., Lake Worth, FL, 1994), suggests that zinc in the environment may contribute to feather chewing and self mutilation syndrome in quaker parrots. He advises that quicklinks should be avoided entirely because of the zinc that they contain. Plastic self-locking cable ties can be used to replace all potentially-hazardous toy fasteners.

Be sure to monitor toy use, or the bird can't be held responsible for how it plays with toys. The amorous quaker will improvise love games with toys. Of course, there will always be at least one "surrogate enemy," for our quaker friends often have temper to express, and if that temper doesn't come out against a surrogate enemy, it will be expressed toward a human or other pet.

The creative quaker can sometimes improvise unsafe behavior with "guaranteed safe" toys. Monitor a bird with a new toy to ensure that it has not created some dangerous way to use the new toy.

Necessary Grooming and Related Warnings

Trimming Wing Feathers

Failure to trim wing feathers can precipitate some of the most heartwrenching tragedies a companion bird and its owner can physically and emotionally endure. From accidental escape to occasional disfigurements on the cooking stove,

being closed in drawers, being sat on, or drowned in a toilet or tub, dangers posed by flight are real and potentially fatal. Having seen the worst-case scenarios, I am convinced of the necessity of careful, frequent, wing feather trims to inhibit flight in companion quakers.

In terms of successful physical and behavioral development, it probably doesn't matter whether a young quaker parrot ever flies. This differs in some other parrots, especially the African gray. Although African gray parrots are considered by many to be the smartest parrots in the world, they are the athletic "nerds" of the parrot world. Like many intelligent species, they are slow to mature. They are clumsy and often fall, which can badly affect the baby bird's physical and emotional health. In order to develop confidence and independence, a baby gray is best

Trimming all ten of the primary flight feathers to within about 1/4 to 1/2 inch (6 to 13 mm) of the next layer of feathers (the coverts) will temporarily ground the efficient quaker parrot flying apparatus.

allowed to—very carefully—learn to fly before it's first wing feather trim.

In contrast, I see little or no need to allow most baby quakers to achieve flight, and there may be compelling reasons why it is better for companion quaker parrots not to learn flight. They are usually emotional "rocks" who are much more likely to learn to chase than to fall. These birds can be little torpedoes and can easily break a neck on the first flight—or slip out through a less-than-quickly-closed door.

Aside from the obvious dangers of a flighted bird encountering a ceiling fan or being slammed in, or escaping through a door, a flighted quaker parrot can incur "dispositional" damage if it learns to use that incredible capacity for flight to attack other individuals.

Complicating matters even further, not all wing feather trims will effectively ground a quaker. Many

times in my dozen-and-a-half years of recapture counseling I have heard: "His wings were professionally trimmed only a few days ago!" from a distressed human whose companion quaker was sitting in a tree! Trimming either only one wing or allowing the end two or three primary flight feathers to remain long will *usually* fail to inhibit flight in a quaker parrot if the bird catches the wind.

Even if a quaker parrot's wing feathers are adequately trimmed to ensure that it will not become airborne, the agile quaker parrot can climb a tree in an instant. Quaker parrots should never be given liberty out of doors, whether or not their wing feathers are trimmed.

A healthy bird enjoying normal molts will probably require wing feather trimming at least three times yearly. Some owners simply maintain the trim by clipping each feather as it regrows. Of course, no feather is ever to be cut through the soft, flexible sheath that indicates blood supply to the developing shaft, but rather a new feather is cut only when it is completely open.

Grooming

Frequent owner maintenance of grooming can be part of intimate, face-to-face play between owner and bird. A quaker parrot will expect a favorite person to groom its neck, a behavior called *allopreening* when it occurs between two birds. Since a molting quaker may have a neck full of painfully stiff new feathers on its neck, a loving owner must gently

Quaker parrots can survive some extremes of climate if dependable sources of food and water are available.

break away the crusty sheath of the new feather. This is probably easier and works better when the feathers are wet.

Beaks and Nails

Quakers love playing Hide-and-Seek in the voluminous, soft folds of a bath towel or blanket. This is the Towel Game. (Variations of this game include Peek-a-Bird, Where's the Bird? and Where's Mom/Dad?)

While interacting directly with the bird during intimate towel games, we have opportunities to maintain the beak and toenails. Quaker parrots can have extremely sharp toenails. Some quaker parrots sharpen their toenails in their beaks or on abrasive surfaces; some quakers blunt file their nails on anything handy. The way a bird maintains its toenails is probably a matter of personal preference possibly influenced by early experience with perches.

Sharp little parrot toenails can cause discomfort to some sensitive human skin, and if humans signal anxiety because of that discomfort, it can provoke the quaker to attack. Well-groomed nails might be an important factor in maintaining a particular bird's tameness. Of course, be careful to nip off only the tiniest tip of a sharp toenail and always have a coagulant powder around to stop minor bleeding.

If a particular quaker parrot demonstrates a desire to blunt file its own nails, that bird might enjoy a cement nail-grooming perch. While I do not advocate this type of perch

When trimming wing feathers, point the scissors away from the bird's body to avoid cutting a tiny toe.

for every quaker, and, especially, I do not advocate installing it as the highest perch—the perch the bird would sleep on—I know that Tza-tza and other quakers that blunt file their nails really enjoy this extra feature.

Likewise, if the bird enjoys sharpening the beak on the cage or accessories, and if the bird has a tendency to nip, a sharp upper mandible can break skin and negatively affect human interactions and confidence. Many a quaker parrot learns to love having the tip of the upper mandible sensitively filed by a favorite human with an emery board. Be sure to support the head on both sides with thumb and longest finger. Support the top of the head and upper mandible with the index finger

To file the bird's beak, support both sides of the bird's head with the thumb and longest finger. Support the top of the head and the upper mandible with the index finger.

Examine the bird frequently so that it doesn't suffer accidents as a result of acquiring flight from newly-grown wing feathers.

Oven Use and Cleaning

To minimize risk to a bird while you are using or cleaning the oven, it is best to have the bird situated as far away from the kitchen as possible and to ensure adequate ventilation around the oven (utilize exhaust fans, open windows, etc.). Even during normal oven use, fumes or smoke may contain tiny particles that, due to a bird's delicate respiratory system, can become trapped in the bird's lungs and cause respiratory distress (rapid or open mouth breathing, coughing, etc.). Regardless of oven type, when cleaning an oven, the bird should be removed from the area and adequate ventilation around the oven provided during the cleaning process. The manufacturer's directions should be followed for proper oven cleaning procedure. If oven cleaners are used, non-aerosol ones are least likely to harm a bird.

Margaret Gaut, D.V.M.

(see page 56). Be careful to avoid damaging the eyes. Be sure to use a nail file or emery board only, as a Dremel (power) tool can be too jarring for a small bird such as a quaker parrot.

Playing the Towel Game occasionally, perhaps twice weekly, with the bird in the towel will maintain a happy, confident, and accepting attitude when the bird is toweled for physical examination. This conditioning to accept toweling could save the bird's life in the future if the bird is injured or ill and must be restrained for medical treatment (see page 59).

Hazards in the Home

Quaker parrots are probably much more likely to be lost to acci-

dents than to illness. This can save lots of veterinarians' bills in a careful home or pile them up in a careless one. It places tremendous responsibility on humans to provide a quaker-safe environment.

Next to flight-related accidents, being crushed is probably the leading cause of death in the companion quaker parrot. These little characters really like to cuddle, and it's not unusual for a bird to snuggle under an Afghan or quilt that might be subsequently sat on with great force. Being squashed or suffocated is an especially common fate among quaker parrots that are allowed to sleep with humans.

Because of their active and curious natures, quaker parrots are vulnerable to being closed into closets and drawers. I once knew a lucky quaker who survived for 24 hours in a closed drawer; it's a good thing that the bird's owner was meticulous about wearing fresh underwear every day, or the bird might not have been found in time!

Like all parrots, quakers are fascinated by water and are often victims of drowning. Be sure to leave the toilet lid down if the quaker has access to the bathroom. Be careful not to leave a half-full glass on the counter beside the quaker perch, for more than one hapless bird has been drowned head first in a glass that was carelessly left in reach. Unattended tubs, sinks, mop buckets, and dishwater have led to many quaker parrot deaths.

Dianalee Deter reports that her quaker parrots love to stick their heads into things: loops of string, too-large cage bars, and other unusual spaces. Sometimes, if the perch is too close to the food or water bowl, one of her quakers will invariably find a way to get its head stuck. Be sure that any loops are eliminated from string, fabric, or leather toys. Rigid rings should be large enough that the bird's whole body can pass through. Replace all small clips, split rings, and quicklinks with self-locking cable ties (see section on toys, pages 49–50).

Roaming, unsupervised companion quaker parrots are less prone to chewing than cavity-breeding parrots, but they are still occasionally vulnerable to various types of chewing accidents. Exposure to lead, especially by ingestion, can be fatal. Common toxins in the home include:

• oven cleaners
• aerosols
• pesticides
• insecticides
• medications
• avocado
• chocolate
• alcohol
• coffee
• diffenbachia

A parrot grooming another parrot is allopreening.

- philodendron
- some other poisonous house plants.

Also, moldy foods are potentially toxic.

Quakers love to play with the same things humans play with, so they are usually very interested in whatever is in the ashtray. Not only can a curious quaker be burned by cigarettes left smoldering, but the bird can be poisoned by nicotine.

Misuse of polymer-coated and -impregnated cookware such as Teflon can kill all birds in the home virtually immediately. Fumes from other polymer-impregnated products such as stove parts, drip pans, coffeemakers, irons, and ironing board covers can also kill a quaker parrot if the product is burned or overheated. If a coated skillet is overheated—over 500°F (260°C)—the fumes will poison the bird in minutes. I have often counseled in homes in which owners were well aware of the danger and owned *only one* such polymer-coated skillet, but not infrequently, this is the *exact pan* chosen by guests in the home.

All but one of the dozen or so polymer fume deaths I have documented have involved inattention related to alcohol use. The story usually goes something like this: A houseguest comes home late after enjoying a few drinks, decides to fix tea or pasta, sits down, and falls asleep leaving the coated pan to burn. The pan catches on fire; the birds scream to warn the humans just before they die.

Inattention caused by alcohol use can lead to a huge variety of bird accidents in the home. If you've been drinking, leave the cookware in the cabinet and the bird in the cage. If you do burn a polymer pan and the bird is still breathing (rare), get it immediately into fresh air and rush it to the veterinarian before its respiratory system closes down. Something can be done if it's done quickly.

Because accidents can happen in the best-meaning households, I advise throwing *all* polymer-coated or -impregnated cookware away. It isn't worth the risk of losing a treasured bird because someone burned a pan.

Injuries from Thrashing

As with other parrots, a quaker parrot can easily injure itself thrashing in fear. This might occur as a result of a cage located where humans or other animals frequently rush past and seem to "appear out of nowhere," as when coming through a doorway or moving around in the dark. In this case, move the cage, call to the bird to warn that you are coming through, or notify the bird that you are with it in the darkness by talking or by turning on the light.

More commonly, however, quaker parrots can injure themselves by thrashing as a response to loud noises, especially loud construction machinery, tools, backfiring automobiles, firearms, or fireworks. Fireworks are especially dangerous in stimulating enough fear to cause a quaker parrot to thrash and injure

Any uncovered water can represent a drowning hazard to a fun-loving quaker parrot.

Coffee can be toxic to quaker parrots.

An aquarium cover can save a quaker parrot's life.

Loose loops in lace and crochet can entrap tiny toes and strangle an unsupervised quaker parrot.

itself. When it is likely that fireworks will be used near the home, try to keep windows and drapes in the bird's room closed and a television with sound on for the duration of the time when they might be frequent (such as on the Fourth of July). This will muffle the sounds of the exploding fireworks and lessen their impact, perhaps, by "tricking" the bird into thinking the sounds are coming from the television.

Medical Care

As mentioned previously, because of its robust constitution and inquisitive nature, a companion quaker parrot is probably more likely to suffer from accidents than from illness. For this reason you must develop a relationship with a reputable avian veterinarian, preferably by visiting the veterinarian immediately after the bird comes home. Additionally, you should know of a 24-hour veterinary hospital or clinic that is willing to treat untimely quaker accidents.

Breaking Blood Feathers

One of the most common minor quaker emergencies is breaking a wing or tail blood feather. As these feathers are molted out and replaced, they are covered with a white or bluish sheath indicating that this is an immature feather with a blood supply. If the feather is broken in the vascular portion of the developing feather, there could be a great deal of bleeding. Since the blood supply is rich in the developing feather, and very constricted at the point where the feather shaft enters the skin, the most effective way to stop the bleeding in most cases is to pull the feather out.

A broken primary wing blood feather can seem pretty scary if the bird flaps and splatters blood on the wall. The first time I saw this I felt I was in some kind of nightmare movie. The first time your bird breaks a blood feather, take it immediately to an avian veterinarian or to the breeder or dealer who sold the bird. They can demonstrate how to safely pull the feather so that you can do it in the future.

Quaker Parrot Home Emergency Kit

• Coagulent powder	First aid powder to stop bleeding
• Pedialyte or lactated ringers	Replaces electrolytes in dehydrated or sick birds
• Hemostat or needle-nose pliers	To pull off broken blood feathers
• Hydrogen peroxide	To disinfect any bleeding wound
• Carrier	To be kept handy in case of fire

Restraining the Bird

To restrain a bird in a towel for grooming, to pull a blood feather, or for veterinary examination, begin by approaching from below rather than above as a predator would. First, confine the bird, then place it approximately in the middle of the towel, grasping it around the neck with one hand, joining the thumb and opposing finger (outside the towel) just under the lower mandible. Even if there is a little space in the circle formed by the fingers, if the fingers are directly beneath the lower mandible, the bird is restrained and cannot bite. Hold the other end of the bird—including the feet—with the other hand, being careful not to restrain the in-and-out action of the breast. Since a bird has no diaphragm, its chest must be able to expand, or it cannot breathe.

Once the bird is safely restrained, grasp the base of the feather shaft with the needle-nose pliers, hold the skin at the base of the feather, and pull the feather straight out in the direction it grows. An immature feather comes out easily. Apply pressure for a few seconds, and the bleeding will stop. Apply coagulant powder if necessary.

Stress reactions to being restrained for emergency treatment can be prevented by desensitizing the bird to towels. A quaker parrot that is socialized with the Towel Game (see page 53) to accept and enjoy handling in a towel will not usually experience an adverse stress reaction to being restrained in a towel when necessary. The quaker parrot that is frequently toweled for grooming is also typically less likely to respond negatively to toweling during veterinary examination and treatment.

Band-related Accidents

Broken legs and other band-related accidents are also not unusual. Many experienced quaker veterinarians will suggest removing a band, especially a loose band, to prevent a heartbreaking accident. Save the band, record the number, and keep both with your bird's records in the event you are ever required to document ownership.

The Carrier

Because of the danger of fire and the quaker parrot's tendency to accidents, always keep the carrier near the bird's living space. If the

Proper towel restraint for grooming and physical examinations is more restrictive than the Towel Game, but doesn't restrict the movement of the quaker parrot's breast so that the bird can breathe.

59

A too loose or too tight band can cause accidents that might lead to amputation or death.

Provide annual or semiannual veterinary examinations, whichever your veterinarian recommends for your particular bird. Quaker parrots are notorious for hiding illness—including sometimes-fatal egg-laying situations—until they are practically dead. If the bird loses weight, becomes listless, stops vocalizing, stops eating, or develops loose, runny droppings, get it to the veterinarian as quickly as possible. Keep an injured or sick quaker parrot warm and quiet until you get to the veterinarian. If a bird is in obvious discomfort, give it Pedialyte or lactated ringers instead of water.

Diet and Behavior

Never underestimate the behavioral influences of diet. Timing and content of diet may be the most influential factors in the prevention and modification of all behavior problems. Examine and enrich a misbehaving quaker's diet; a bird on a boring, inadequate, or erratic diet probably thinks it has good reason to complain or to be naughty.

Feeding on a schedule is especially beneficial in preventing unwanted vocalization. Quakers like to eat at least twice daily, morning and evening. Quakers also enjoy eating with humans, but, if they are fed by hand as they beg from the human table, you will see their gathering behavior.

carrier is buried somewhere in the back of a basement or attic, there will be difficulty reaching the carrier as well as emotional resistance by humans to getting help for an injured bird. Dr. Margaret Gaut, a Williamsville, Illinois, veterinarian suggests practicing fire drills to see if all gear is ready and available quickly. When taking the bird to the veterinarian, Dr. Gaut says, "It is best to take the entire cage, if possible, without having to clean or remove anything from it."

A wild quaker foraging in an abundant field will pick up one piece of food after another, take one or two bites, and drop the food. If they can get to it in the future, they will "graze" on the food they gathered earlier. This can be unhealthy behavior in captivity where the bird may spend quite a bit of time in one place, soiling anything underneath with droppings. If a bird is handed one piece of food at a time at dinnertime, the perch must be cleaned before it spends time there again, or it could get sick from the soiled food. When eating with a companion quaker it's best to give it limited quantities of food placed in the bowl at the same time humans are served their meal.

Feather condition, including the way the bird maintains its feathers, can also be an indicator of the quality of the diet. Broken, dull, or chewed feathers might easily signal the need for an improved diet, for the key to good feather condition is building strong feathers with balanced nutrition. This is usually easy to accomplish in a normal, healthy quaker parrot with any of the quality commercial diets available today, supplemented with fresh foods.

From years of watching feral quakers in the Rocky Mountain area, I have become convinced that quaker parrots enjoy, perhaps even need, something resembling grit in the diet. Oyster shell calcium is eventually digested, but oyster shell

Trapping a Feral Quaker

I had been repeatedly contacted by staff at a huge health maintenance facility that had been recently built in a landscaped and partially wooded alpine meadow. They reported that throughout the winter a small parrot would often huddle up beside the sheltered, sealed second-floor windows.

One particular nurse had continued to call about the parrot that visited their facility every midday. My suspicions about what type of parrot was living wild in the Denver area were confirmed late one morning as I watched a large, hearty quaker parrot eating mud alongside a stream through the partially snow-covered meadow.

By feeding the bird and establishing a food dependency, the sympathetic support personnel had done half the job of capturing the lone creature. Placing my own quaker parrot, Tza-Tza, on the Preview-Hendrix 125 cage/trap squarely in the center of a large patch of snow, I waited behind a shrub to pull the door closed behind the bird. It took only a few moments from the time she noticed Tza-tza until she flew to the cage, and only moments thereafter, she clamored into the cage for brunch.

The recaptured bird responded quickly to friendly handling and was eventually adopted by a pediatrician in the facility.

grapes, mangoes, collard greens, carrots, and squash.*

Dr. Jerry LaBonde suggests a diet of "no more than 40 percent commercial diet"** combined with lots of fresh, unseasoned human food. My quaker parrot, Tza-tza, enjoys just a little low-fat Mozzarella cheese and some warm, good-quality whole grain toast every morning with his fresh fruits and vegetables.

Manufactured Diets

When providing a manufactured diet, consider mixing about 5 to 10 percent small seeds such as a canary-and-millet-based mix. Do not use seed mixes that include sunflower or safflower for quaker parrots. I see several advantages, behavioral and otherwise, to including at least a small amount of small seed in the quaker parrot's regular diet. Some quaker parrots enjoy digging around in the food bowl and examining the size and shape of each morsel of food. The also enjoy the tactile pleasure of cracking seed. Accommodating these behaviors can help to prevent a variety of behavior problems from unwanted vocalizations to feather chewing.

When using a good-quality manufactured diet, be sure to purchase the formula for companion birds. If you are feeding the manufactured diet designed to stimulate breeding

Never underestimate the behavioral influences of diet.

with granite, readily available in bird supply stores, provides both additional calcium and a little grit.

Calcium

As with other parrots, quaker parrots need a ready source of calcium in the cage, but other minerals are needed too. In the wild, dirt is probably a handy source for the many minerals needed to keep the quaker parrot's body working properly. The need for multiple minerals may be the reason many quakers demonstrate a preference for cuttlebone over calcium blocks. Cuttlebone is often a more diverse mineral source, as it can provide magnesium, iodine, and other minerals that might not be added to some calcium blocks. Dr. Greg Harrison suspects that quaker parrots have a sensitivity to salt and suggests that they avoid high sources of salt such as human junk food, canned corn, fruit cocktail,

---

* Greg Harrison, DVM, telephone interview, 1997.
** Jerry LaBonde, DVM, interview, 1996.

behaviors, you will see escalating biting, screaming, and other behaviors associated with breeding. On the other hand, when rehabilitating a neglected bird, the enhanced nutrition provided by a breeding formula might be needed temporarily to overcome molting or health problems.

Vitamins

Resist the temptation to supplement vitamins without the supervision of an experienced avian veterinarian; in some situations, excess vitamins can kill a bird more quickly than too few vitamins. Be sure to not supplement vitamins if you know that the bird has a history of liver or kidney problems. The nutrients provided by real food—particularly when combined with a modern, scientifically formulated commercial diet—are more beneficial and less dangerous than supplementing vitamins.

Withholding Food

A quaker parrot on a truly deficient diet might not have the energy or motivation to do much of anything. Withholding food is a particularly cruel and also inefficient way to modify quaker parrot behavior. It is far more effective to distract the bird from unwanted behavior before it occurs.

Water

Of course, every parrot must have constant access to clean, fresh water. Many troubling physical as well as behavioral problems can

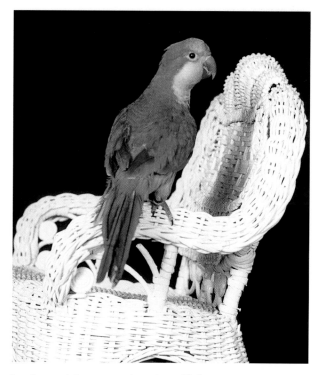

be traced to no water, insufficient water, or dirty water in the bird's environment. Although quaker parrots are known to quickly foul water in a dish, offering water in a dish or bowl is much preferred over a drinking tube. Most quaker parrots bathe frequently when provided with a large enough container of water. Then, of course, the dirty bath water must be changed, but the presence of the water for bathing contributes to the prevention of attention-demanding behavior and self-mutilating behavior.

If, on the other hand, a particular quaker parrot is obsessed with immediately dumping all the water out of its bowl every day, and there

Feather condition can often be improved with diet.

is fear that the bird's health might suffer from lack of water through the day, then a drinking tube must be provided. In this situation, the bowl of water is a "tool" for allowing the bird to continue its daily "watering" ritual (which may be a remnant of a healthy wild behavior).

Working for Food

In the wild, most parrots spend more than 90 percent of their time foraging for and consuming food. If they have to work for it, then the resulting behaviors are predictable and appropriate. For example, a quaker parrot might benefit behaviorally from having to remove corn from a whole cob, perhaps with husks still intact. Provide eggs and most fruits (preferably organically grown) unpeeled for maximum behavioral benefits. Like playing, eating is a truly self-rewarding behavior.

Chapter Six

Occasional Problems and Their Control

Real and Threatened Aggression

Quaker parrots in the wild exhibit little actual territorial-related aggression toward known individuals of their own kind and they often allow storks, opossums, bats, or geese to share their large communal nests.[*] Paradoxically, companion quakers are famous for developing and expressing aggression in their home territory. Whether defending a cage (physical territory) or a person (emotional territory), they are known to do so with intense determination. The following handling and environmental manipulations will augment patterning to the step-up command and transportation dependence to ensure a quaker's good disposition.

- Control aggression in the cage by frequently rearranging perches and toys.
- Control excessive bonding-related aggression by balancing bonding and not allowing the bird

to become emotionally fixated on one particular human or territory.

- Always remove the bird to service the cage.
- Don't insist that a quaker come out of the cage on the hand; allow the bird to climb out of that fiercely protected compartment onto the door or top of the cage where it will sweetly comply with the step-up command.
- Move the cage and play areas at least twice yearly; the more time the bird spends in one place, the more violently it will defend that space.
- Take the bird on frequent outings into unfamiliar indoor territory: the bank, the stairwell, the laundry room.

An astute owner soon learns to differentiate between actual and threatened aggression.

---

[*] Matthew M. Vriends, Ph.D., interview, 1992.

If all humans interacting with the well-patterned bird use the same handling techniques, the bird will respond to all humans appropriately.

vocalization; however, it does have a well-deserved reputation for being able to learn to make some pretty obnoxious sounds. Therefore, reasonable residential sound-proofing and/or understanding neighbors may be necessary in high-density living situations.

As with any parrot, a quaker must vocalize regularly, but the raucous scream of the wild quaker is learned behavior and does not usually appear in hand-fed birds raised by humans. It's easy to reinforce a quaker in non-screaming behaviors, especially when humans are present.

- Teach all humans expecting to handle the quaker parrot to use appropriate techniques and procedures.
- Don't allow the bird to chase another living thing. Intervene if this happens, whether the bird is being provoked or is provoking another animal or human.
- Help the bird to express nervous energy by providing opportunities for exercise, including frequent drenching showers.
- Don't house the bird higher than anyone's head, and don't allow the bird to dominate children from a higher position.
- Don't allow a poorly patterned quaker parrot to sit on a human shoulder, especially a child's shoulder.

Excessive Vocalizations

The quaker parrot has neither an extremely loud voice nor a reputation for excessive frequency of

The quaker parrot's natural tendency to learn human speech can be used to replace noisy behaviors. Redundant annoying sounds like "Ak (pause) Ak (pause) Ak" are more likely to develop in the quaker parrot than actual screaming. I believe we often observe this behavior if food, fresh water, or favored humans are physically or emotionally absent. If the bird begins a pattern of repeating an annoying noise, we prompt the bird to say something or make a sound we do like, and reward the bird for replacing the annoying sound with the acceptable one. Ideally, we distract from this redundant "Ak" before it occurs on a given occasion, stimulating and reinforcing any inoffensive behavior. This might be a nice time for a shower. A bird saying *Ak...ak* is trying to attract attention; most birds don't want to attract attention when they are busy resting, rezipping feathers, or are vulnerable because they are wet.

What Do I Need a Secretary For? I Have Nicki!

Many of us champion socially responsible causes. While some folks concern themselves with Saving the Whales, or Feeding the Children, my own passion is the Demise of Telephone Solicitation. *I'm not interested in death-to-the solicitors, but to the invasive and inconsiderate interruption of my private time through the telemarketing trend in business.* I have a busy psychotherapy practice, and write articles and books in my spare time. Phone calls break my train of thought, but I must answer the ring as it may be a patient in crisis.

By contrast, Nicki, my quaker parrot, really enjoys the telephone and often adds his two cents' worth to my conversations. My little green companion frequently joins me in the evenings, and his favorite perch is my left shoulder. That's precisely where he was last night, as I was working on an article for a parenting magazine about positive and negative reinforcement of behavior.

The phone rang. I placed it to my right ear and heard an unfamiliar sing-song voice say, "Good evening, and how are you tonight?"

My work was stalled, and my radar was on. "Are you trying to sell me something?" I asked.

"Oh, no!" came the voice on the other end of the line. "Because of your outstanding credit, Bank X has raised your credit line. Congratulations. We are offering you an opportunity to...."

As I was trying to think of the most effective means of negatively reinforcing this telemarketing behavior, Nicki spoke distinctly into the receiver from his vantage point on my shoulder. *Oh, Stop it! Stop it!*

Dead silence on the line; the caller hung up.

Clearly, the solicitor got the message.

Pat James Baxter, LPC, LMFT

If a companion bird picks up a bit of profanity or somehow comes up with an inappropriate word, try not to accidentally reinforce this unsuitable behavior; laughter may be the primary facility by which this type of behavior is accidentally reinforced. The attention garnered when humans react with anger or scolding will also reinforce the behavior, so it is better to try to ignore the behavior until a plan for its replacement can be implemented.

One approach is to find a similar-sounding word or group of sounds that are just as much fun for the bird to say, then model and reinforce those appropriate sounds. For example, if a quaker picked up the word *dammit* and we were offended by this particular word, we might quickly instruct associates and family

Distract a quaker parrot from making annoying sounds before they commence.

The laughter of the favorite human may be the strongest reinforcer of behavior in the companion quaker parrot.

their birds at night as a means of controlling when the bird perceives "daylight." Most quakers seem to match the daily routine of the household and seldom start normal morning calls before human flock-mates arise.

Toys Can Help

Toys, including bells, moving parts, and shredable rope, can be the first line of defense in preventing the development of boredom-related behavior disorders that include screaming and feather chewing. Play is a very desirable behavior. It is self-rewarding and easily learned by a bird that isn't reinforced to expect constant human handling and attention. Be sure the toys are small enough to be safe and easily enjoyed by a small bird.

members to frequently use and rein-force the words *can it* for the bird to copy. If the bird gets more attention for *can it* than *dammit,* the inappro-priate word or phrase will soon be replaced (but not forgotten).

Quaker parrots don't usually vocalize loudly in the dark, so noise control can be almost instantly accomplished by covering the cage. To prevent sunrise sere-nades, some quaker owners cover

Don't underestimate the allure of even very simple toys like paper towel or tissue bows (to be system-atically removed) or coffee stirrers, straws, or twigs (to be arranged or woven into "nests"). Not only is a busy quaker a happy quaker; a busy quaker is also not screaming.

When a Quaker Parrot Doesn't Talk

It's almost unheard of for a well-socialized, hand-fed domestic quaker parrot to not learn at least a dozen human words. These birds almost invariably learn to say *Step up, Nite, nite,* and almost anything else they hear frequently. I've even had reports of humans hearing escaped birds say *Step up* to attract attention to be recaptured. When a hand-fed domestic quaker parrot doesn't talk, we usually find that the bird was housed only with birds that did not speak, was isolated from humans for the first couple of years, or (*very* rarely in quakers) is expressing the consequence of ill health or depression.

We can usually defeat failure to talk in a young domestic quaker with increased handling, improved modeling, and adding full-spectrum light and other environmental enrichments. Some birds may fail to talk because they are housed too low and don't wish to attract attention. Merely raising the bird and demonstrating the joys of increased attention will often produce words—maybe practice words—almost immediately. Of course, improved handling techniques may be required to offset increased aggression that comes as a result of raising the height at which the bird is housed.

Like other parrots, a quaker will practice sounds it is learning at low volume. It's not unusual for humans to fail to recognize a talking quaker parrot because they can't hear or understand them. In this case, we must improve modeling and reward for improved understandability.

When a quaker parrot stops talking it might be reverting to "bird talk" as bonds to humans lessen and bonds to birds increase. This might be a natural consequence of the introduction of another quaker. It is

Nicki tries to get the phone to talk back.

one of the reasons I favor one-quaker homes and feel that we will enjoy the best companion qualities in homes with *only one* quaker parrot.

A quaker parrot might stop talking because it is ill, injured, or experiencing stress related to the desire to breed. If a good-talking quaker suddenly stops talking, it should be

Toys can be the first line of defense in preventing boredom-related behavior problems.

A variety of experiences will stimulate the quaker parrot to happiness behaviors, including talking.

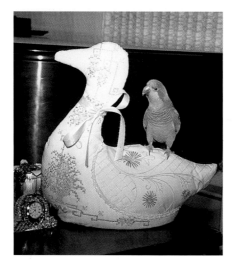

result of isolation, poor diet, loss of a favorite human, or loss of a favored companion animal. Depression in a quaker parrot might even result from something innocuous like a new light fixture or piece of furniture that the bird doesn't like. Some birds are especially concerned about the introduction of lamps, noisy or invasive clocks, humidifiers, oscillating fans, or ceiling fans. This is a stress reaction and may be accompanied by other stress reactions such as feather chewing. It is unusual, however, in a bird that has been conditioned to accept change.

taken immediately for evaluation by an avian veterinarian.

A quaker parrot might stop talking because it is depressed. Although this is very rare in quaker parrots, depression can come about as a

We might temporarily move or remove the offending inanimate object, or we might try to desensitize the bird to the device by familiarizing the bird with the object. We might leave the fan in the room for

Quaker parrots kept with other quaker parrots often prefer to speak their own language rather than human language.

a few days before we turn it on, we might leave a ceiling fan or light fixture on the floor for a while so that the bird gets used to its appearance, and we might use the bird's name in tandem with the object— "This is Zeke's fan"—to further desensitize the bird.

A quaker parrot might also discontinue talking as a result of the addition of a new pet or baby. Again, we work to desensitize the bird to the new family member, using their names in tandem: "Zeke's baby" or "Baby's Zeke." Leave puppy or baby toys and accessories around the house for a few weeks before the new arrival, and tell the quaker parrot who (or what) is coming. After the new arrival, be sure to give the quaker increased attention for a time and be watchful for opportunities to reinforce appropriate behavior. Temporarily raising the height of the bird's cage can also help to offset this problem.

Molting

A couple of times every year, but especially in the fall, a normal quaker parrot will probably wind up with a neck full of something that looks like hard little spikes of carpenter's glue. These are pinfeathers or new feathers that still have the blood supply. As each feather matures, the white covering hardens and flakes off as dander or feather dust.

Expect to see these new feathers appear soon after you notice that

there are more feathers to be cleaned up off the floor and cage bottom. (Birds molt out of old feathers at about the same time dogs and cats are shedding.) The bird may be both nippier and noisier than usual.

There will probably be an unavoidable tendency for humans to wish to avoid handling the cranky quaker. This is a time for more attention to detail in handling the bird so

A quaker parrot might be annoyed, offended, or depressed when confronted with a new object in the environment.

Increased attention and handling can overcome many behavioral problems.

Many quaker parrots enjoy having humans "groom" the new pin feathers on the back of their necks.

have enough wing to fly within about a month, and, since quakers are excellent flyers and famous "escape artists," their wing feather trims must be more frequently maintained than those of some other birds.

As the feathers grow out, they will be provided with blood supply in a flexible white sheath. Wing and tail feathers in this condition can be easily broken. A broken wing or tail blood feather will result in bleeding. If the feather is dripping blood, it must be pulled or it will continue to bleed. (See the medical care section on pages 58–59 for instructions on how to pull a broken blood feather.)

If the bird is kept in a temperature-controlled environment, some relief for incomplete or difficult molt might be found in sunny, warm afternoons outdoors or the addition of a little heat and full-spectrum light indoors. Retained feather sheaths on the head and neck can be softened with "rainfall," and sensitively removed by human or avian buddies.

that humans do not get hurt, and, if the bird is handled less, the contrary behaviors will worsen. Thus, when the bird is cranky it needs *more* attention than usual, not less. The "attention" might not be direct handling if the bird resists or attacks, but it might come in the form of more showers, a more exciting variety of foods and toys, increased vocal interaction, or eye games and passive interaction.

When the bird drops neck and body feathers, it will usually also drop wing and tail feathers. When we see the bases of those cut wing feathers lying on the floor, we know that they will soon be replaced by full, new wing feathers. Pick the feather up, and make an appointment with the groomer. The bird will

Feather Problems

Feather chewing is unusual in baby quaker parrots, although a domestically bred baby quaker parrot, especially if it was parent raised, might come with chewed feathers on the head. Since the bird can't reach its own head feathers, the presence of chewed feathers on the head is an indication that the bird was chewed by parents or companions.

But any quaker parrot, even a baby, can develop feather chewing as a response to illness; therefore, any indication of feather chewing should first be examined by an experienced avian veterinarian. If the bird is causing damage to skin, we must consider that the behavior may be a result of physical illness. A quaker parrot suffering from physically generated self-mutilation involving skin may require a collar or protective appliance to prevent self-injury. While these devices may be helpful in preventing damage during physical recovery, they are of little benefit behaviorally and are to be avoided when treating most behavioral feather chewing.

Quaker parrots occasionally develop feather problems that start as a result of poor quality or old feathers, much of which is related to unsuccessful completion of the molt. Behavioral feather shredding can also arise, however, from any form of damaged feathers. A very snuggly bird might wind up with oil-damaged feathers from being petted too much with oily or sweaty hands, or lipstick-damaged feathers from being kissed too much. Behavioral feather shredding might result if the bird overpreens or tries to "even up" damaged feathers. This may be either a cause of or a response to stress.

The Influence of Diet

Never underestimate the influence of diet. Be sure the bird has a diverse, interesting diet and that the

When we see the bases of cut wing feathers lying on the floor, we know the bird will soon have full new wing feathers.

diet is offered on a consistent schedule. Consider increasing protein and calcium levels at least temporarily so that the bird can produce better feathers. Be sure to offer oyster shell calcium, grit, mineral blocks, and cuttlebone. As mentioned previously, avoid giving your parrot salt.

Although less common, a feather-shredding quaker might be excessively active. If the bird is overly high-strung and/or underweight, we might manipulate the amount of hemp in the diet from 2 to 3 percent up to maybe 6 to 7 percent, or even eliminate hemp entirely. Evaluate the behavior of the bird after increasing or decreasing the hemp when considering further manipulations. We also increase opportunities for exercise, especially including rainfall (showers), as a means of expressing underutilized energy.

Lighting

Don't forget that birds need full-spectrum lighting to properly assimilate calcium. The duration of light during the day might be as significant as the quality of light. Consider increasing or reducing the duration of daylight to manipulate feather chewing.

Abandonment

Behavioral feather chewing, shredding, or plucking can also appear as a response to perceived abandonment. As discussed in Chapter Four, we teach our companion quakers a concept of time so that we can tell them when we are going away and reassure them that we will return.

Response to Human Stress

Behavioral feather damage can appear as a response to human stress in the home environment. Marriage, divorce, pregnancy, alcoholism, drug addiction, illness, depression—all can generate stress and stress reactions in the companion quaker. These influences must be addressed to remove or neutralize the stress they create before we can expect improvement in the bird. Because quaker feather chewing can escalate to self-mutilation syndrome, it's best to seek professional medical and behavioral assistance immediately.

Sexual Stress

Feather shredding or chewing may be related to sexual stress in some cases, but it usually occurs in a mentally and physically understimulated bird. If the feather-shredding quaker is insufficiently active and slow to complete the molt, I might consider offering a little extra thyroid nutrition and sources of vitamin A. I have seen excellent results from the addition of Ethical Nutrients Thyro Vital and Spirulina powdered and dusted on moist foods and combined with an enhanced environment and behavioral program. Again, we might manipulate the diet to increase metabolic activity levels. Enhance nutrition primarily with real foods, avoiding vitamin supplementation because of the danger of vitamin D_3 toxicity.

Manipulating the Environment

Success in training the bird away from habitual behavioral feather shredding or chewing can often be accomplished by manipulating elements of the bird's environment. Any activities that cause the bird to move will ultimately assist in the stimulation of the bird's metabolism, which can lead to the resolution of the problem. A bird that is hanging upside down bopping its toy is not overpreening and shredding feathers. A bird that is showered every day will not be chewing off feathers when they are wet, and wet feathers are an opportunity to reinforce non-chewing behaviors.

While we might temporarily increase the temperature at which the bird is housed, we must be careful to not subject the bird to hot, dry, direct forced air. Be sure the bird is housed well away from heating ducts. If we try to facilitate the molt by raising the temperature, we must also carefully monitor moisture and/or increase bathing.

Toys

Be sure to include multiple toys of different types so that the bird has

Determination

After Maxine and Paco's first clutch of babies, I pulled their nest box to give them a rest. Maxine had proven to be an excellent mom, but because she was a "rescued" bird, I tend to spoil her a bit. Needless to say, she had different ideas.

When Max is upset, she "beats up" her favorite toy, her Polly-Dolly. Several days after the nest box came down, I noticed that the rope portion of her toy was on the bottom of the cage, along with a few molted feathers. Paco is building again, I thought. That same evening, the pair was doing their "cluck-dance" in the corner near the makeshift nest. Not again!

Two days later there it was—a new egg, carefully laid on the piece of shredded rope.

Janice A. Wagner
Charlotte, North Carolina

the opportunity to choose which toys to play with. Just because a bird doesn't play with a particular toy doesn't mean it "doesn't like toys." It means that the bird isn't interested in that toy at that time. Unless the bird is afraid of the toy, the toy's presence provides an opportunity to exercise confidence-building, decision-making processes. As previously mentioned, avoid anything such as quicklinks that may contain zinc.

Consider allowing the bird to have increased height, including possibly, enough wing feather to fly

Many different types of toys provide a bird with confidence-building opportunities for decision making.

until the behavioral feather chewing can be resolved. As confidence increases, aggression, activity, and independence increase, and feather chewing declines. If a baby quaker is housed too low, reprimanded too severely, or not allowed to develop

Wet feathers can help to reinforce non-chewing behaviors.

at least a little "attitude," the loss of confidence could result in a sedentary bird. A quaker with an understimulated metabolism overpreens, resulting in feathers with split ends that are eventually chewed off.

Eye Games

Manipulating eye contact as well as playing passive eye games can improve confidence in an anxious bird. Try playing Peek-a-Bird around the corner, the Blink-Back game, and "I can hold still longer than you can." Treat feather chewing in a shy bird by improving any elements you can identify that build confidence. As the bird's confidence increases look for more nips and tail wags (perhaps keeping a record of the number of happiness behaviors observed each day), and the feather chewing will stop.

A quaker parrot that begins destroying its own feathers needs professional assistance immediately. Feather mutilation can be progressive and life threatening. Dr. Steven Feldman of Denver, Colorado, reports that he has seen a self-mutilating quaker that came within a millimeter of severing its own jugular vein. He has also seen a quaker parrot that *did* sever its own jugular vein.

Allofeeding

As with other parrots, allofeeding (regurgitating) is one of the most common early sexual behaviors in quakers. Even at a very young age, a happy, amorous quaker may wish to provide the object of its affection with warm, gooey, partially digested food.

To a bird, this is romantic behavior—and quaker parrots can be *very* romantic. To a bird being courted, this behavior says, "Look what a good parent and provider I could be! I could do a great job of feeding your babies!"

Humans may be less than excited by the deposit of something resembling warm oatmeal in their hand, hair, or ear. Obviously, this behavior must not be reinforced, lest the bird decide that the way to win friends and influence toys is by feeding them.

We occasionally see a bird with the vice of feeding everything, including perches, in the environment. This can be very messy.

With allofeeding as with other behaviors, distraction and reinforcement of the introduced behavior will redirect the behavior. For example, when a bird starts feeding the owner's hand, simply say, "Be a good bird! Go play with your toys!" Put the bird down and ring its bell in its face until it gets interested in playing with or attacking the bell. We might hand the bird a tiny holding toy, maybe one of those little plastic barrels with a moving bell inside, then tell the bird it's a "good bird" or a "pretty bird" when it performs the distraction behavior.

Once again, the laughter of the favorite person is probably the

When keeping more than one quaker parrot, expect to see more sexually inspired behaviors.

strongest reinforcer of this type of behavior. If you laugh when Zeke feeds your hand or the telephone receiver, you might have to clean up a lot of goo during all the remaining days of your (or the quaker parrot's) life.

Other Sexual Behaviors

Masturbation

The arrival of sexual behaviors might be signaled when either gender begins allofeeding a toy or other objects or begins rubbing against toys, cage, or perch, or their companion's hand, head, or other body parts seeking sexual fulfillment. Expect a male quaker to form a consummated relationship with his bell. Some cocks pleasure themselves often, sometimes sounding more like a snake than a little green bird. Most male birds will probably masturbate with the tail pointed down. Most hens will probably do so with the tail pointed up or straight back, but there are many variables here, and tail position is not always an accurate indication of gender.

Just because a quaker parrot masturbates doesn't necessarily mean that the bird is actually interested in breeding; it's not unusual for a quaker parrot to prefer masturbation to copulation. Choice of mate may play a part in this, but probably, in most birds that prefer masturbation, this behavior is a matter of sexual preference that will not change no matter how many attractive mate choices are offered.

Feather Shredding

Feather shredding appearing under the wings of a mature quaker may be an indication of sexually induced stress (see pages 74–75). Since the bird's sexual organs are under the wings, just behind the thighs, petting or other stimulation under the wings can activate breeding behaviors, including allofeeding, masturbation, egg laying, and sexually induced stress reactions such as feather chewing.

Egg Laying

A quaker hen can begin laying eggs before the age of three. It is usually a rare occurrence in a companion quaker with no sexual partner. Of course, humans may be petting the bird in a way that the bird finds sexually stimulating, and, while it is not especially unhealthy for a hen bird to lay an occasional egg, it can have adverse effects on her disposition.

Examine the amount of protein in the diet. Ideally, that level should probably be somewhere between 10 and 16 percent. Any time protein levels exceed 16 percent, we can expect to see an increase in all sexually related behaviors.

Excessive egg laying can deplete even the strongest constitution. A companion quaker that is producing more than half a dozen eggs in a cycle should be seen by a veterinarian who can provide hormone therapy or perform a hysterectomy. If the bird has gone more than three days since the last egg, remove all the eggs so that she will not be tempted to develop the vice of eating her eggs.

Solutions

Of course, any sexually stimulating activities must be discontinued. The bird must be given projects and activities to distract from sexual behaviors. These can include increased showering and bathing, exercise, enriched environment, and better attention to speech training and patterning rituals. This might be a good time to give the bird a pop-up box of tissues to ravish or a whole box of coffee stirrers to haul and throw around. Be sure the bird has an appropriate surrogate enemy toy to beat up.

Both masturbation and egg laying can be treated with manipulation of light. The quality, quantity, and duration of light all can influence these behaviors. Especially consider manipulating the length of the artificial "daylight" periods the bird experiences.

A good-quality light source provides full-spectrum light. A hen, especially, requires full-spectrum light as part of the process of absorbing and utilizing calcium. This is particularly important for an egg layer. One hen might be laying because she is getting too much light for too long periods during the day, while another might be laying because she is getting too little light and has found a dark corner to crouch in—another activity that can stimulate sexual behaviors. Of course, manipulating the light would mean decreasing light for one bird and increasing it for the other bird. This is a trial-and-error situation; you may have to experiment to find the correct solution for a particular bird.

Retrieving a Lost Companion Quaker

Dr. Jerry LaBonde, who serves the largest avian veterinary practice in Colorado, has been heard to comment, "If it's flown away, it's probably a quaker."

Indeed, in the vast Denver metropolitan area I have captured many, many free-flying quakers, including one—of absolutely unknown ownership—only blocks from Dr. LaBonde's office.

Hand-fed baby quaker parrots are completely dependent upon humans for food, water, and other survival necessities.

In states where they are allowed, quaker parrots are the largest of the frequently escaped companion hookbills (budgies, lovebirds, cockatiels, and quakers). Of that group, they are also usually the most easily recovered. Since hand-fed domestic quakers have always received their food only from humans, they are usually completely dependent upon humans to provide food and water. "Recapturing" a hand-fed quaker parrot is, therefore, no more complicated than reaching the bird and offering food or giving the step-up command.

When a hand-fed domestic quaker flies away, we must work quickly and try to keep the bird in sight. If we stay with the bird, when it decides to go to someone, we will be there, and the bird will come to us.

An escaped hand-fed quaker parrot usually goes to a human by dark the first or second evening it is out. By the second day, the lost

Helping Mattie Sue

On December 20, Mom got a call from her friend Mattie Sue, a bird recapture specialist. She asked if my brother and I would like to help a boy in Parker, Colorado, find his quaker parakeet that flew away at 4:30 that afternoon.

It was still dark when Mattie Sue picked us up the next morning. Her quaker parakeet Tza-tza and her dog Jessie were in the van. It was still dark when we got to Parker. It was also very cold, about 10°F [-12°C]. We walked around the yard in the dark, and we went next door to the fire station. Then we went inside the boy's house to warm up. When the sun came out, we all went back to the fire station. We told them about the lost bird. The fireman let us put up a lost bird flyer drawn with crayons on notebook paper.

We paired off and went searching around the neighborhood for the bird. We searched in fields, on hills, and in pine trees. We didn't see or hear him. Mattie Sue and one of the big kids heard some bird sounds around bird feeders, but we still didn't find him. We went back to the house to warm up, and Mattie Sue drove us home. Whew—boy, were we tired!

Mattie Sue went back that afternoon with computer-made signs on bright paper, and a woman called to return the bird within an hour. The bird had flown four blocks away to the yard of a home with many cats, a cockatiel, and another quaker!

Brendan Kullback, age 8

quaker should be very hungry and very ready to find a friendly human.

Even the nastiest quaker is often quite pleasant to a human who takes it in from the hostile, scary, and sometimes cold outdoors. There is occasionally a temptation on the part of a human finding the bird to simply keep it. Rescuers are sometimes knowledgeable enough to be judgmental about an owner who doesn't trim the bird's wing feathers. Depending upon the owner's intentions and practices, this might be a justifiable criticism. It is, therefore, important for the owner to report the missing bird to police and animal control and to offer a reward for the bird's return. This demonstrates the owner's honorable intentions and dedication toward the bird.

A quaker that wants to be charming can be really, really charming. If the bird is being very sweet to its newly chosen human, we might even have to offer a reward to get it back that exceeds the material value of the bird.

If we lose sight of the bird, everything is much more complicated. When we don't know where the bird is, the whole project becomes a public relations job. We must advertise that the bird has been lost, offering a reward for its return. Brightly colored flyers posted around the neighborhood are much more effective than white ones. Newspaper advertising, including both area-wide and neighborhood press, is often very effective.

I suggest advertising at least a $50 to 100 reward for the bird's return and small rewards for any information about the bird's whereabouts. For the latter purpose, I carry $2 bills when tracking a bird. These bills are a novelty, and the children treasure them, but be sure to give money to children only in the presence of their parents.

Children are absolutely the most diligent and vigilant scouts in finding a loose pet bird flying around the neighborhood. If we can keep the children in the area looking for the bird, we have eyes everywhere.

Not everyone who finds a lost companion parrot is honest. It's not uncommon for a less-than-scrupulous stranger holding the lost quaker "for ransom" to have an exaggerated notion of the bird's actual material value. I like to mention on the flyer that the bird is somehow imperfect, and therefore not especially valuable. With an older bird I might say that the bird is known to attack or that it has daily medical needs. I believe information of this nature can generate faster and more reasonable response if the bird has fallen into unscrupulous hands.

If we know where the bird is, and it is in a high, inaccessible place, we can sometimes lure it down with a

LOST PET BIRD

KIKA

a QUAKER PARROT
Lost on DECEMBER 20
near Safeway
in Parker, Colorado

Has special dietary needs

REWARD
for Return of the Bird

SMALL REWARDS
for any Information
Leading to His Return

**Call Jane Doe at 321-555-1234
if you see this very beloved
pet bird**

A sample flyer for use in finding a lost companion quaker.

like bird, food, or jealousy. Sometimes the presence of the person the quaker parrot hates most will bring

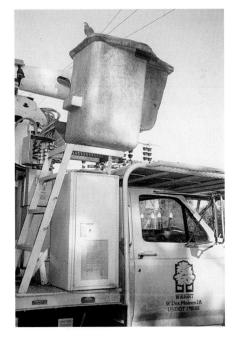

A cherry picker is the safest possible climbing accessory.

Food dish is lowered on movable shelf until the bird must enter the cage to get the food and a human waiting out of sight pulls the door closed with a wire.

the bird down sooner than the presence of the most beloved person. Especially if the favorite person is expressing affection to the most hated rival, the bird will sometimes come down more quickly because of jealousy than hunger.

If you have to climb a tree or other structure to get close enough to reach the bird, be sure to take a pillowcase with you. It's hard enough to hold onto an angry, full-flighted quaker, much less climb with one. Just tie the pillowcase in a knot to contain the bird and drop it carefully to a helper on the ground. If you must climb, be particularly careful when using metal ladders around power lines. Electrocution is probably the most common cause of death or serious injury in an accident occurring during pet bird recapture. The safest possible climbing accessory is a cherry picker, a large piece of tree-trimming equipment used by a professional operator.

Avoid the use of water hoses for the purpose of capturing a free-flying quaker; these birds are excellent fliers, even when wet. It's highly unlikely that a good-flying quaker

can be prevented from flying with water from a garden hose, and the pressure of water from a firefighter's hose could kill the bird. On the other hand, those huge "Supersoaker" water guns can shoot a stream of water up to 50 feet (15 m). If it's dark or the bird is tiring, it can sometimes be "herded" or harassed to lower and lower places with the water gun.

Although capturing a free-flying, hand-fed quaker might be as easy as walking up and saying *Step up!* recapturing an experienced, human-wary wild-caught quaker can seem a gargantuan task. The easiest way to capture a good-flying, human-shy bird is to first establish a food dependency, then trap the bird. A trap can be easily made from a manufactured parrot cage lying on its back with a movable wire rack that can first be situated at the (top) door to the cage. Place food first on a white dish on top of the cage. Each day, move the shelf lower into the cage. Within a few days, the bird will have to go into the cage to get the food, and the door can be pulled closed, trapping the bird inside.

Behavioral Intervention

If humans in the environment are being repeatedly outsmarted by a cantankerous little tyrant quaker parrot, professional behavioral intervention might make a world of difference. Amazingly, a quaker that cannot be touched by anyone in the house will often prove perfectly cooperative with a professional stranger. Sometimes, only one session with a parrot behavior consultant can turn a monster into a saint. Owners may be stunned, moved to tears, and comment that they "don't recognize" or "don't know" that precious creature (with just a tiny remnant of yesterday's blood on the tip of its beak).

Look for a professional parrot behavior consultant with quaker experience. Ask a reliable avian professional—a veterinarian, breeder, or other quaker owner—for a local referral for an in-home consultation. If there is no competent local behavioral counselor to provide help for a misbehaving quaker, telephone counseling, although more time consuming, can be a reasonable alternative. If you must depend upon telephone counseling for behavioral intervention for a quaker parrot, be sure that the bird behaviorist works in a state where quakers are legal so that that person will have a body of hands-on quaker experience from which to draw. Since there is little formal education in the area of managing companion quaker behavior, I believe the consultant with the most quaker experience will be most likely to be able to successfully adjust the bird's behavior.

Expect the consultant to take a behavioral history and evaluation to determine what changes are needed and how to generate them. Then, an objective outsider with a little more experience and a little extra attention

Sometimes only a professional outsider can regain control of a poorly-socialized quaker parrot.

to technique can often teach quaker owners to defeat an unappealing behavior in a matter of minutes.

We must carefully evaluate both the bird and the bird's surroundings to determine whether something is missing in the bird's physical or behavioral environment. The bird might have simply learned to get attention with inappropriate behavior. A normal, stubborn animal might be confusing the owner with incomprehensible behavioral messages. The bird might have been poorly socialized as a nestling or only slightly socialized as a baby. It might be in an inappropriate or under stimulating environment. In any event, the bird is trying to accomplish something with its behavior.

Most companion quakers respond dependably to predictable environmental or handling manipulations: rewards, bathing, eye games, step-up training, petting, exercises, etc. Once favorable behaviors are generated, they must be reinforced. Behaviors receiving sensitive intermittent reinforcement usually become redundant, habitual behavior.

Depending upon the age of the bird, we probably have a window of opportunity of two to seven days to reinforce introduced changes. If the bird returns to exactly the same physical and behavioral environment, the behavior will return to what it was before. This likelihood increases with increased age in the bird.

Although the bird's behavior isn't actually "permanently" changed by behavioral intervention, the benefit of demonstrating immediate changes can be the turning point in the attitudes of humans who create the bird's environment. Because behavior is difficult to change, "quick fixes" that are used to demonstrate what a companion bird is capable of may be the best way to convince humans that if they change *their* ways, *the bird's* behavior will also change. That's a bigger *if* than it sounds. It's a real temptation for a behavioral counselor to train the bird and stop, but if humans are not adequately trained, the intervention may be unsuccessful, even though the bird responded perfectly.

Humans working to improve companion quaker behavior must also understand that a behavior cannot be eliminated, but, rather, a behavior must be replaced with a different behavior. That is, a bird that is biting when given the step-up command cannot simply *not* bite. It can, however, replace the biting behavior with a well-patterned and accurately executed step-up command (in a quaker, this is often accompanied by a verbal *Step up!* from the bird).

Behavior isn't linear; that is, it comes and goes. A behavior that is being eliminated will not suddenly stop. It will stop (in response to behavioral manipulation), then reappear, then stop, then reappear. If the behavioral intervention is working properly, each reappearance of the unwanted behavior will be of shorter duration and less intensity. There will be an ever-increasing number of happiness behaviors, and the unwanted behavior will gradually disappear.

Abuse

Some abuse of companion parrots by humans is intentional and meant to hurt the bird. In my opinion, however, the vast majority of abuse of companion parrots by humans is probably unintended abuse and perpetrated in the name of "teasing," "play," or "punishment." Most humans probably have a family heritage of owning companion mammals (usually cats and dogs) or raising children. Each of these types of experiences are with creatures that have evolved as predators, so their responses differ from the responses we would expect to see from a prey species such as a quaker parrot.

"Playing" as Abuse

Bouncing a rubber toy on a string moved rapidly in front of a normal kitten's face will provoke a pounce—an act of hunting. This behavior is a sign of good health and happiness in a kitten, a predator. Birds, however, are prey species, as can be observed from their eyes, which are situated on the sides of their heads rather than in the front. Instead of the instinct to hunt, these creatures have an instinct to fight or fly, with an accent on the fly. Because they must be able to escape from predators, these prey species have developed the ability to see almost 360 degrees around the head rather than merely see the area in front of the head.

Given the opportunity, when threatened, most birds probably prefer to fly away from danger. In a

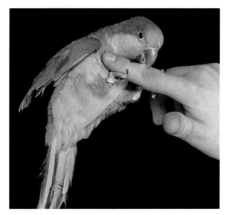

If humans aren't properly trained, even the best trained quaker parrot might revert to inappropriate behavior.

bird such as a healthy companion quaker parrot with trimmed wing feathers, if the bird cannot fly away, the instinct to fight will dominate the instinct to fly. This might make it seem that a provoked quaker parrot that is defending itself or its territory is enjoying jousting with the broom handle or golf club. Actually, the strong emotional reaction (fear) that the bird is feeling is probably quite unlike the emotions felt by a kitten in the act of hunting (joy). Defending its territory from a large predator may indicate health on the bird's part, but it is a stress reaction, not a happiness behavior. Therefore, provoking a quaker parrot to defend its territory (a stress reaction) is ultimately destructive to the bird's health and personality, and is, therefore, abusive.

Provoking the Quaker Parrot to Chase

While some quaker parrots appear to relish chasing people away from the cage, I believe this behavior is also a stress reaction.

Provoking a quaker parrot to bite or attack can be a form of behavioral abuse.

Repeatedly running past the cage can cause recurrent stress reactions and ultimately harm the bird. Therefore, if family pets, children, or others frequently rush past the cage, stimulating either fear, thrashing, chasing, or attacking in the bird, the cage should be relocated. If the cage is beside a doorway that people rush through, it can seem to the frequently terrified bird as if they are magically appearing out of thin air. The cage should be moved or humans should move more slowly or be more careful to notify the bird vocally if they are about to come through the door.

Humans who intentionally provoke a quaker parrot to chase must be advised that their behavior is abusive. An adult who is teasing or provoking a quaker parrot can easily choose to stop. If children or companion animals are abusing the quaker parrot, they are probably best denied access to the bird (especially if the bird is also "abusing" them). If these situations cannot be quickly remedied, the bird should be removed from the home.

Punishment

The quaker parrot is a willful and determined animal. It is a wild, undomesticated creature that cannot help but use the tools nature has given it. A human who cannot tolerate an occasional bite is probably not cut out to be a parrot owner. Hitting the cage, throwing things at the cage, blowing smoke in the cage, or spraying anything but a mist of water (rainfall) at the bird can very quickly damage the bird. Hitting a quaker parrot, "thumping" it on the beak, throwing the bird on the floor, or against the wall, can easily injure or kill the bird. A nipping quaker is most successfully patterned using the techniques and responses described in this book and handled more or moved to a more empathetic environment.

I occasionally encounter people who have withheld food from a quaker parrot because they have been bitten. This is especially cruel and insensitive, as a quaker parrot does not have the mental capacity to understand that it is hungry today because it bit someone yesterday.

I once did an in-home for an "aggressive quaker parrot" where the owner admitted that the bird had been given no food since biting about ten days before my visit. When I advised that the bird should be immediately given food, the owner proceeded to fill the bowl with black oil sunflower seeds (the kind bought cheaply at the grocery store for feeding wild birds), the bird's exclusive diet. Not only had this particular owner figured out how to overtly abuse the bird by withholding food, he had destroyed the bird's health by feeding it a grossly inadequate diet. Obviously, the bird didn't have much energy by the time of my visit, as it had survived by eating the shells from the sunflower seeds (and who knows what else) foraged from the bottom of the cage. I recommended placing the bird up for adoption.

Neglect

Failure to feed for behavioral reasons is, unfortunately, a common scenario for a quaker parrot that is about to be given away. If the owner has decided that the bird is incompatible or untrainable, it might not be fed again in that home. This is especially common in situations where the bird has been banished to a basement or backroom because it is noisy, messy, or otherwise unappreciated. Obviously, the bird must be removed from the home immediately.

It is not uncommon for such a bird to consume surprising amounts of food during the first few hours in the new or foster home. If food deprivation has been ongoing for some time, the bird might have physical problems related to chronic malnutrition or might develop a permanent behavioral problem with overeating. A chronic overeater must be carefully monitored to avoid the development of obesity.

Positive interactions rather than punishment are effective in establishing appropriate behavioral habits.

Secret Abuse

While a quaker parrot that is suddenly deciding to attack a certain adult, child, or other companion animal probably is not responding to secret abuse, suddenly becoming fearful and avoiding a child or human might indicate that secret abuse is occurring when the human and bird are alone. Multiple subtle behavioral changes such as overeating, thrashing, fearfulness, discontinuing talking, increased vocalization, avoiding a particular individual, or ripping out feathers only in that individual's presence could be signs of secret abuse.

It's time to spend a few moments investigating the source of the behavioral changes. In some cases, the bird might be the subject of secret abuse, but this is not always, or even often, the case; in most cases it is probably no more than a temporary response to an accidental behavior. Feather chewing, especially, is a very complex physical and/or behavioral

A quaker parrot should be encouraged to interact with many different individuals, including close friends and strangers.

Scapegoating

Not all of life goes as we expect, and nothing ever stays the same. Difficulties in human relationships can sometimes result in the quaker parrot being blamed for human problems. If the bird is either causing human problems such as pain, allergies, or sleeplessness, or if it is being blamed for human problems, especially if physical or emotional abuse is occurring in the home, the bird must be removed from the home immediately.

condition that does not, in itself, indicate that a bird is being abused. Some of the most pampered, obviously unabused birds in the world chew their feathers.

Temporary Foster Care

Many life changes and transitions are temporary. If it seems that a situation will improve, it's comforting to know that the bird can come home some day. For this purpose, I like to encourage quaker parrot owners to encourage their birds to have relationships with an appropriate foster parent or family. This can provide a quaker parrot with potential vacation housing, improved relationships as a result of balanced bonding, and a place to stay during times of personal transition.

Permanent Adoption

If the situation creating abuse for a quaker parrot is not going to change, a permanent adoption is necessary. Because of what the bird has been through and the behavioral responses to those problems, a potential owner should not be expected to pay anything resembling a retail price; however, the new owner should be expected to pay for the veterinary evaluation and any behavioral and physical rehabilitation. If the new adoptive owner has an appropriate cage, the bird should be given *without charge* to the new owner. If the new adoptive owner does not have an appropriate cage and the current owner does, then the current owner might suggest a modest price for the bird's cage and accessories.

Chapter Seven

Rehabilitation

The Previously Owned Quaker Parrot

For a person seeking a free or very inexpensive bird, there are usually frequent opportunities to rehabilitate previously owned quaker parrots. While many birds, especially older wild-caught or recaptured ferals, offer only limited companion potential, young adoption or resale hand-fed birds are good candidates to become quality companions.

The Physical Rehabilitation Process

An adoption or resale quaker parrot with good companion potential is probably no more than two or three years old. Radically improved behavior is possible at any age, but it is especially easy at this age. This is a common time for an unsocialized quaker to be bounced to a second home. A quaker parrot that has not been handled can become a real tyrant in its home territory. Moving the bird will make a big difference.

While the quaker parrot is not usually a shy creature, changing homes can be unsettling for even the most cantankerous animal. If the bird was not socialized to accept change, the move could be extremely unsettling. The perceived drastic changes provided by coming to a new home usually provide a window of opportunity for reinforcing good behavior during the temporary period of adjustment. This is similar to the "honeymoon period" experienced by baby handfeds coming into the first home, but the window of opportunity for reinforcing good behavior is brief. You must work quickly and decisively to make the most of this fleeting opportunity.

An adoption quaker may not have had the best care, so begin the

Even well-behaved, perfectly feathered quaker parrots are sometimes available for adoption from homes in transition.

When taking home a new parrot, immediately examine and update the bird's wing feather trim.

physical rehabilitation process by taking the bird immediately to the avian veterinarian, possibly before you ever take the bird home. Be sure to observe appropriate quarantine procedures as specified by the veterinarian, especially if there are other birds in the home. This period will probably be at least one to three months, during which time the quaker must be behaviorally rehabilitated. If behavioral rehabilitation is not begun until after quarantine, we may have already missed the window of opportunity to easily reinforce appropriate behavior.

Ask the veterinarian to examine and update the bird's wing feather trim. This will be important in training or retraining the bird to step up. During the first few hours or days in the home, a little extra security can be provided by covering about one fourth of the cage with a towel so that the bird has a place to hide if it chooses to do so. Place the cage well out of traffic areas and a little

higher than you normally might. If there are no other birds already there, situate the bird in the living area for resocialization.

If the bird can be handled, hold it as much as possible during the first 48 hours. Work on step-up patterning (see pages 17–19) for as long as you and the bird can stand to do it. Handle the bird less if it seems to tire easily, perhaps providing a little extra heat and privacy for the first few days.

Even though the bird should have no strongly developed instincts to defend new territory, be sure to practice step ups outside the bird's new home territory. Be sure also to pattern the bird to step up on a handheld perch as well as onto hands. Never attempt step ups from the cage unless the bird is well patterned to step ups in unfamiliar territory.

A two-to-three-year-old quaker parrot in a new home should go through a "honeymoon period" similar to the baby days followed by the terrible twos just as a baby quaker would, but these developmental phases will be of much shorter duration. A young, adopted, domestic bird should be socialized exactly as a baby quaker would.

The Adopted Quaker's Diet

When the bird's diagnostic tests come back, consult the veterinarian before trying to improve the bird's diet by supplementing vitamins. If the bird has a less-than-healthy liver or kidneys, be very careful about vitamin supplementation, especially with D_3, which could kill the bird. It is better to improve the diet with real food: fresh fruits, vegetables, pasta, and a quality commercial diet. Almost any food—quality whole grain toast, macaroni and cheese, or oatmeal—served warm should seem like "love" to a previously hand-fed quaker parrot that has been neglected. Don't forget to offer minerals such as mineral blocks, cuttlebone, and oyster shell calcium.

It's not unusual for a newly adopted quaker parrot to be addicted to seeds, especially sunflower or safflower seeds. This is similar to adopting a child that will eat only French fries. It's important to get these birds on a canary-based mix as quickly as possible; then we can begin mixing the pelleted diet with the seeds and eventually wean the bird to healthy food.

Games

As quickly as possible, the bird should be socialized to enjoy the Towel Game (see page 59). A bird that has been mishandled may be terrified of the towel. Try to use a light green towel; that would be the same color as the bird. The goal here is to replicate the feeling of security of being under Mommy's wings.

If the bird is initially afraid of the towel, try playing with the bird in the covers of the bed. Blankets may be less intimidating to a bird that has been roughly toweled.

Warning. Be sure not to fall asleep when playing snuggle games with the bird in the bed.

Wild-Caught Quakers

Because of its international status as an agricultural pest rather than a threatened or endangered species, the quaker parrot was the last bird legally imported into the United States. The last legal wild-caught quaker parrots entered the United States in 1993. If these birds live to their thirties, there will be older wild-caught quaker parrots occasionally in the marketplace in

Don't attempt step-ups from the cage until the bird is well-patterned to step-ups in unfamiliar territory.

Provide your companion quaker parrot with a nourishing diet.

Silly eye games are an excellent way to establish and maintain an emotional connection with any quaker parrot.

the United States through the year 2023. Wild-caught quakers will probably continue to be available outside the United States.

Although older and possibly never before socialized to human touch, a surprising number of these birds may offer good pet potential. They require the same veterinary examination and quarantine, and they experience the same stages of behavioral development as a domestic baby parrot as they acclimate to the new home. The same socialization processes used with handfeds should be used for wild-caught quakers, but changes and advances should be made more carefully, with this exception: A new handfed baby quaker parrot should be held on a limited schedule only, guiding it to learn also to play alone (develop independence). An older, bird-bonded or wild-caught quaker parrot should be held for long periods of time to build and improve the human/quaker bond.

Rather than beginning with touching and holding, however, the new owner should begin befriending an untamed parrot with games and passive interactions as discussed in my book, *Barron's Guide to a Well-Behaved Parrot*, pages 17–21. It is best to establish contact with the bird first with games that involve no eye contact and progress to games involving limited eye contact. Offer food from the hand, play the Towel Game, and sleep in front of the bird before hand contact is attempted. Again, if the bird won't tolerate the Towel Game, try playing Peek-a-Bird with a blanket, bedspread, or quilt.

Many tamed, wild-caught quakers bite less than their domestic cousins. Tamed wild-caught quakers sometimes fail to acquire human speech, but they can be charming companions in a different, wilder way.

Old wild-caught quakers are often available through adoption programs with bird clubs. In many cases, the only way to identify a resocialized wild-caught or feral quaker from a resocialized handfed is by the open band and by the voice. A quaker parrot that has been around wild quaker parrots may come with a totally obnoxious voice. It may be necessary to spend more time on noise control than actual socialization, but don't neglect socialization just because a quaker makes a little noise. A conscientiously applied program of increased handling, combined with distracting from the noise *before* it occurs and reinforcing the introduced behavior will quickly bring the noise under control.

Recaptured Feral Quakers

Some may argue that feral quakers established in the United States are happy living in their wild state and should be left alone. In some situations, however, there may be compelling reasons to recapture. The birds might be living in an area where they would be subjected to extreme or adverse weather conditions, or they might be in danger of being exterminated to protect agriculture in an area where they might proliferate. As nonnative species, there is no protection for this bird, and no reason why a citizen, especially a farmer, couldn't kill the bird.

While a recaptured feral quaker probably has the least potential of this group to learn speech, many of them adjust well to life in the living room. They will probably be addicted to seed and will probably require "taming" to get the hang of the step-up command. I have tamed and taught step ups to many such birds, and it's usually much easier than one might suppose.

As with wild-caught quaker parrots, begin befriending an untamed quaker parrot with games and passive interactions. Again, start with games involving no eye contact and progress to games involving limited eye contact. When it has calmed somewhat, take the wing feather-trimmed bird to a small restricted area such as a bathroom, closet, or hallway. Begin the first day by sitting on the floor with feet drawn up and knees up. Put the bird on a quaker green towel on your knees and spend an hour or so reading out loud to the bird. The second day, spend less time reading, and begin socializing with the Towel Game, progressing as quickly as possible to the step-up command.

Even an older quaker that has lived wild on more than one occasion will frequently tame down in minutes. Again, the biggest battles here will probably involve reducing noise and improving the diet.

When a Quaker Parrot Survives Its Owner

A quaker parrot that is acquired late in a human's life will probably survive its owner. When a quaker parrot survives its owner, there is usually a very brief period, usually no more than a few weeks, of silence or withdrawn behavior. A quaker parrot that loses its owner rarely stops eating; more likely, the bird will become truculent and territorial and not allow anyone near its cage. It might call or continue looking for that favorite person. Likewise, a quaker parrot might mourn, call, or seek out a recently deceased household pet.

This is one more time when the existence of a second or foster home that is willing to become a permanent home is ideal. If the bird is already familiar with the new permanent human and new permanent home, the transition will be easier. The bird's diet and routine should remain as close as possible to the one it was before the loss. To make the transition easier, owners should provide a written record of the

A quaker parrot might mourn the loss of another long-time companion animal.

only is this good for the solitary owner, it also ensures that the bird will be found should the owner fall ill or die. Because it takes only a short time for a bird to die of thirst, a check-up system is necessary to ensure its survival. This service for the elderly might be provided through a church volunteer organization or other in-home service provider; it is a noble and worthy project occasionally available through local bird clubs.

bird's customary diet, preferences, dislikes, and vocabulary as well as information about the bird's veterinarian, groomer, behavioral consultant, pet sitter, boarding facility, or other service providers, and any other idiosyncrasies that might affect the bird's happy adjustment in a new home. This written record might resemble the information recommended for a physical and behavioral history form in the section that follows on operating a quaker parrot adoption program.

Owners who want to know where their birds will go if anything happens to them should make arrangements today. If there is no established foster home, or no provision for the bird in the owner's will, the bird might be placed through an adoption service.

If a quaker parrot's owner is ill, elderly, or otherwise homebound and lives alone, it's a good idea to establish a daily "check-up" system so that someone knows that all is well in the house every day. Not

Operating a Quaker Parrot Adoption Program

It's been said before: Nobody's perfect, and nothing stays the same. The quaker parrot is one of the birds most frequently transferred through adoption programs in the United States. Many absolutely "normal" neglected quaker parrots are given away through adoption programs every day. Even the best-loved companion quaker might someday need a home.

Many local and American Federation of Aviculture affiliated clubs operate adoption placement programs. Most of these programs are operated by volunteers and are free of charge, although the program might request a donation from both the person placing the bird for adoption and the person adopting the bird. However, operating an adoption program can be one of the most troubled areas of any organization. Some of the most bitter disputes and misunderstandings I have ever observed have developed as a result of adoptions.

Nowhere in aviculture is there a greater need for record keeping. At least three documents are needed to complete and record each adoption:

1. *Application to Adopt a Quaker Parrot* from a potential new owner;
2. *Physical and Behavioral History* from the current/former owner; and
3. *Transfer of Ownership* to the new owner.

If there is an interim need for temporary care for the bird (a foster home), five documents are required to complete the transfer of ownership to the new home:

1. *Physical and Behavioral History* from the current/former owner;
2. *Transfer of Ownership* to the individual or organization supervising the adoption;
3. *Agreement for Foster Care* between the care provider and the individual or organization supervising the adoption;
4. *Application to Adopt a Quaker Parrot* from a potential new owner; and
5. *Transfer of Ownership* to the new owner.

Advance Screening of Adoptive Homes

Because it is desirable that the bird go quickly and directly into a permanent new home, it's a good idea to accept and review applications for potential new owners before the birds become available. The following information at least should be included on an *Application for Quaker Parrot Adoption*. It's a good idea to have your organization's forms reviewed by an attorney.

• Name/Address/Day and Evening Telephone
• Please describe your previous experience with parrots.
• Have you ever owned a quaker parrot?
• Where is that bird now?
• What other companion animals, including birds, do you now own?
• Do you now have an appropriate cage for a quaker parrot? What are the cage dimensions?
• Have you read *Guide to a Well-Behaved Parrot* or other behavioral manuals?
• Are you willing to assume all responsibility for this bird?

A written record of a quaker parrot's preferences will make transitions to new homes easier.

Many quaker parrots exhibit strong preferences for particular types of music.

ion, it should be adopted into a breeding situation.

Following are suggested considerations for the *Behavioral and Medical History* form:

• Name of quaker parrot:
• Band number and type of band:
• Original source of the bird:
• Age/hatch date:
• Time in this household:
• Anomalies or identifying characteristics:
• Eating habits:
• Playing habits:
• Bathing habits:
• What does the bird say?
• Have you observed any extremely fearful behaviors regarding humans? Animals? Objects? Restraint?
• Preferences (foods, music, gender, color, etc.)
• Has this bird ever been injured or ill? Describe:
• Has this bird seen an avian veterinarian? Who?
• Are you willing to have veterinary records transferred?
• When was the last time the bird went to the veterinarian?
• Has the bird had any behavioral problems including shyness, screaming, biting, or self-mutilation in the past?
• Has this bird seen a behavioral consultant? Who?
• Are you willing to have behavioral records transferred?
• Does this bird have a regular groomer, pet sitter, or other regular service providers? Name and describe:

• Do you intend to maintain this bird as a companion or a breeder?
• Do you have experience breeding quakers or other parrots?
• Are you familiar with the Model Aviaries Program?
• At what date are you prepared to assume responsibility for this bird?
• Are there any additional considerations that might affect this adoption placement?

Matching the Bird to the New Home

The needs and characteristics of the bird will affect the home into which the bird should go. If the bird is bonded to humans, it should be adopted as a companion bird. Similarly, if the bird is an egg eater, a chronic masturbator, or has abused its mate, it should be adopted as a companion not a breeder. If the bird has a history of successful breeding and failure to thrive as a compan-

- Does this bird have any physical or behavioral conditions that would affect its ability to reproduce, such as a physical imperfection, masturbation syndrome, egg eating, infertility, previous health compromises, etc.?
- Please list any additional conditions affecting this bird:

This history is true and complete to the best of my knowledge.

(Signature of Current/Former Owner/Address/Telephone)

Transfer of Ownership

If the quaker parrot is going directly to the permanent new home, the only further document would transfer ownership from the current/former owner to the new owner. At least the following suggested elements should be included in a *Transfer of Ownership* form:
- Name of person(s) called "current/former owner":
- Name of person(s) called "new owner":
- Name of individual or organization supervising the adoption
- New owner agrees to assume all physical and financial responsibility for the bird:
- New owner understands that the bird is adopted in as-is condition and neither the current/former owner, the temporary care provider (where necessary) nor the individual or organization supervising the adoption is liable for any preexisting or developing physical, medical, or behavioral conditions affecting this bird or other birds in the household:

- New owner agrees that this bird shall not be sold at any time in the future, and that if lifestyle changes require that the bird find a new home, the individual or organization supervising this adoption will select and supervise the adoption:
- Date and time of transfer of ownership:
- This agreement should be signed by all participating parties.

The Foster Home

If there is no permanent home available for the bird and it must be removed from the present home immediately, then temporary housing—a foster home—must be provided until an appropriate permanent home can be found. This makes things much more complicated, since there is always a possibility of accident or illness or other misfortune in the temporary foster home.

Following are minimal suggested considerations for the *Temporary Care Agreement.*
- Name of bird:
- Name of temporary care provider:
- Name of individual or organization supervising the adoption (new owner):
- Name of person responsible for financial obligations for the bird while it is in temporary care:
- Temporary care provider agrees to quarantine the bird from all other birds for a period of at least one month.
- Temporary care provider shall not be held liable in the event of illness,

Empathetic foster care can often turn a misbehaving quaker parrot's life around.

injury, death, or other mishaps occurring during temporary care.

- Temporary care provider agrees that current/former owner and individual or organization supervising the adoption are not liable for illness, injury, death, or other mishaps occurring as a result of the temporary foster care.
- Conditions under which temporary foster care can be terminated by either the temporary care provider or by the individual or organization supervising the adoption:
- Date and time at which care of the bird is transferred to the temporary care provider:

Agreement should be signed by temporary care provider and the individual or organization supervising the adoption (new owner).

The Permanent Placement

Usually, the *Temporary Care Agreement* will terminate when a new permanent home is found. At that time, a *Transfer of Ownership* form can be provided to document the time and date of the new owner's responsibilities. Careful written records will prevent the vast majority of misunderstandings from occurring during adoption placements. I have never seen a serious misunderstanding relating to a well-documented adoption, and I have seen many serious and bitter misunderstandings that developed during unwritten, handshake adoptions.

Chapter Eight
The Perfect Imperfects

Among the most cherished of all companion quaker parrots are those called "imperfects" in the feather fancy. These are birds that have survived injuries resulting in temporary or permanent disfigurement. They may be available for free or for contribution to their medical expenses. In some birds, the damage is merely cosmetic; in others, the injuries result in reduced capacity to function independently. The plucky quaker parrot is capable of surviving extremely disfiguring injuries. Some quakers have been so badly injured that they have lost important skills such as the ability to walk, fly, climb, see, or eat, yet they have survived to become very happy, successful companions.

Recoverable Injuries

Many of these injuries occur either in the nest box or during hand-feeding. While some of the injuries to baby quaker parrots are permanently disfiguring, it is not unusual for a baby quaker to completely recover from injuries incurred before weaning. Recoverable imperfections include feather-chewed head or back, burned or punctured crop, chewed-off toenails, or spraddle leg (see page 100) discovered within the first few days of life. The baby bird will usually grow feathers on the chewed head or back right away. It is rare, if the feather follicles were damaged, for the bird to not grow feathers in these areas.

Damaged crop. This can occur when a baby quaker is being hand-fed and the formula is either too hot or has hot spots because it was not stirred properly. If the injury is not sutured, the baby will probably die. If a baby quaker survives a burned crop, and the crop was professionally sutured, the adult bird will probably retain no visible signs of the injury. Occasionally, the bird may have some discomfort where the

Imperfect quaker parrots are among the most cherished of all companion birds.

crop and skin over the crop adhere. A badly burned crop might require suturing more than once. Rarely, one or two feathers covering the crop might grow in the wrong direction on the adult bird.

Punctured crop. This is a similar, usually less severe injury that can result perhaps from using cedar chips in the nest box or brooder. Or, a baby quaker might occasionally puncture its crop with a toy or with the clasp that attaches the toy to the cage. Because there is less damage and the skin at the edges of the wound is stronger, this type of injury is usually easier to treat and heals more quickly than a burned crop. With appropriate veterinary care, quaker parrots usually recover completely from this kind of injury.

Spraddle leg. Some baby quakers are hatched with this splayed-leg condition. If it is recognized early, it can usually be partially or fully corrected. The veterinarian may use hobbles or a technique involving pulling the baby's legs down through a customized sponge. These devices hold the baby's legs in a corrective position as it grows while allowing the baby to use the legs and develop muscles. The bird's legs will stay under it in adulthood.

Uncorrected spraddle leg. This might result in the affected leg being "frozen" in an almost unusable position out to the side of the body. These birds must be supplied with an environment especially designed to accommodate their injuries—perhaps by living in a car-peted aquarium, a short, padded box, or a cage with horizontal bars.

Cosmetic Imperfections

Loss of toenails. Many injuries that result in permanent disfigurement don't interfere in the bird's ability to function normally in captivity. One of the most common of these injuries in quaker parrots is the loss of toenails, a common injury among parrots that are shipped or housed in groups. It is also sometimes observed as a nest box injury, as parent quakers may occasionally chew one or more toenails off babies in the nest box. Two or fewer missing toes or toenails are hardly a handicap for a quaker parrot.

Wings, beaks, eyes. Occasionally, a quaker parrot might have suffered an injury that results in crooked or missing wings, a malformed beak, or asymmetrical eyes. While these injuries can result in permanently noticeable imperfections, they do not interfere with a quaker parrot's ability to function normally as a companion to humans. Slightly damaged wings that remove the capacity for flight might be fatal to a wild quaker parrot. In an indoor-living situation, however, a quaker parrot with this kind of injury may be able to have a beautiful set of full wing feathers with no danger of flying away.

One of the most commonly seen beak malformations is called scissor beak in which the upper mandible

This quaker parrot functions normally even though it lost some or all of every toe as a nestling.

and lower mandible are offset to opposite sides. This and some other minor malformations of the beak can sometimes be corrected by massaging or filing the beak into shape. If the bird can crack seed and eat independently, this is really no disability at all. There is anecdotal evidence to suggest that parrots with minor beak deformities are less susceptible to the development of feather chewing and self-mutilation syndrome.

Imperfections that Impair Abilities

Some more severe imperfections may require environmental and handling accommodations such as padded surfaces, wide, flat-topped perches, cages with horizontal bars, or special diets. Perhaps the most common of these is the quaker parrot that is missing all its toes. Again, this is a nest box injury usually caused by a parent bird. Although it

is generally believed that parents that remove feathers from the babies' heads and backs are eager to go to nest again and are merely "persuading" the current babies to leave the nest, this does not appear to be the source of the behavior of removing the babies' toes. A small amount of anecdotal evidence suggests that removing toes may occur more frequently in pairs that breed in nest boxes only rather than weaving some sort of nest or a woven nest in and/or around the nest box.

Colorado breeder Ginger Eldon had a quaker parrot pair that produced perfect babies in a nest box with a woven millet stem nest. Later, when they went to nest without weaving the millet stem nest inside the nest box, they neatly chewed off all the toes (up to about the first joint) from the feet of two clutches of babies. After that, Ginger incubated the pairs' nine eggs per clutch and hand-fed the babies from day one. The Eldons still have two quakers

Don't Forget the Bow

One Fourth of July I was called upon to take a one-legged quaker with a broken leg to the veterinarian. The poor young bird had reacted with great fear upon its first exposure to the sounds of fireworks. Since Colorado is a state that requires banding, the bird's only leg was banded, and, apparently, the band was caught on something in the cage when the bird thrashed in fear in response to nearby explosions.

What a sad sight that little critter was, holding on to the side of the cage with her beak. The owner was consumed with grief and guilt. He vowed never to touch another firecracker.

Dr. Jerry LaBonde removed the bird's band and set her leg in a tiny little splint. He advised me that the bird should stay in an aquarium for a couple of weeks, and that she should have lots of padded hori-

Peg recovered completely from having broken her only leg.

zontal ladders to sit on in the future. Dr. LaBonde was just about to put her back into the cage, when he stopped and looked, and said, "Oh, my, I nearly forgot the bow!"

"Bow?" I asked. "You need a bow on a quaker's splint?"

"That's the most important part," the good doctor replied as he double-knotted a tiny gauze bow. "I call them 'teasers.' If the bow sticks out and maybe moves around a little bit, the bird will chew on the bow and leave the splint alone."

with chewed-off toes from those two clutches. When they were babies, carpet was put on the bottom of the cage of these birds, but now they function as normal adults (even to the point of attempting copulation) in an ordinary cage. These birds still have a little of every toe, but quakers that have only little round feet with absolutely no toes often do just as well.

Quakers that are raised around larger birds must be carefully super-

vised and meticulously housed to prevent altercations. Quaker parrots involved in altercations with larger birds might end up missing one foot or leg (or more). A quaker parrot missing only one foot or leg can still get around pretty well, especially if easy climbing opportunities are provided. Many ladders, flat perches, and horizontal bars should be included that allow the bird to use its beak as a second foot.

Extreme Imperfections

A quaker parrot that attacks a larger bird may come away from the encounter with no beak. Often, this type of injury involves only the upper mandible, in which case the beak can occasionally be reattached by an experienced avian veterinarian. Even those birds missing both the upper and lower parts of the beak often learn to eat independently by scooping foods that don't have to be cracked or chewed. Warm cereals such as grits and oatmeal are excellent for this purpose. Small pieces of fresh fruits and vegetables sprinkled with generous amounts of a good-quality ground pelleted diet can be very effective in providing balanced nutrition for the bird. Loss of the beak may not impair talking ability, although it might affect the motivation to speak.

Blindness: Cataracts in quakers are rare, but we see occasional blindness in them. Even birds that are completely sightless often learn to adjust to their cage, probably through trial-and-error, sound, and vibrations. In these cases, owners should seldom make any changes in the bird's environment. A quaker parrot with sight in only one eye is more common. In this case, we must approach the bird only from the sighted side to avoid either fearful or aggressive responses.

Missing extremities: The extremely adaptable quaker parrot

Imperfect quaker parrots are often considered by their owners to be absolutely perfect in every way.

is well known to survive even some very devastating injuries such as missing both feet or legs. Again, a carpeted aquarium or very short-sided box is good for housing these birds; a footless or legless quaker should not be in a box with high sides it can't see over. According to Dr. Jerry LaBonde, a quaker parrot housed in a too tall box might feel that it's in a hole and develop related behavior problems.

Behavior

The most significant thing about physically imperfect companion quaker parrots is that they often develop extremely accommodating, cooperative personalities almost naturally. If a rare behavior problem does develop, it is usually corrected—as in the "perfect" quaker parrot—with enhanced environment or increased handling. Interestingly, physically imperfect quakers are often considered by their owners to be "absolutely perfect" in every way.

Chapter Nine
Family Issues

Children and Quaker Parrots

Because a quaker parrot is sturdier than a budgie, lovebird, or cockatiel, and yet small enough to do little real damage to a child, it might be the very best choice as a companion parrot for a child. There is great potential for highly complementary relationships between quakers and children, especially between only quakers and only children. Unfortunately, there is also potential for quaker parrots and children to abuse one another.

The best candidates for juvenile quaker owners are tolerant, responsible children who are usually at least six to eight years old. Of course, this

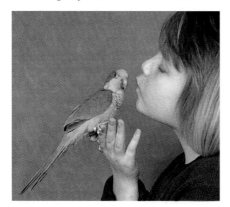

Confident, tolerant children are good candidates for quaker parrot ownership.

consideration is highly subjective and depends completely upon the bird and the child. Some very young children have been able to develop and maintain excellent relationships with quaker parrots. One two-year-old might do very well with a particular quaker, and a teenager might not do well with the very same bird, or vice versa.

Careful training of children to perform step-up practice, and adult supervision of the development of the authority-based relationship are necessary to ensure a peaceful quaker/child relationship. The bird must be patterned to demonstrate the same cooperative behaviors with the child as it would with the child's parent. It is especially important to instruct a child not to teach the bird to chase by running away from it. A timid, fearful child who retreats or runs from the bird can actually provoke a quaker parrot to more abusive behavior.

Because a quaker parrot can perceive children and shorter people as easily dominated and, therefore, worthy of abuse, children should be taught to give the step-up command from a height-dominant position. That is, never try to "hand" a quaker parrot from a taller person to a shorter person, but, rather, place the bird in a lower position than the person who wishes to handle the bird. The easiest way to do this is to place the bird on the floor so that even the shortest person can easily accomplish a successful step up.

It is usually difficult for a child to persuade an established quaker parrot to step up from inside the cage. Instead, children should be taught to give the step-up command to a quaker parrot that has come out of the cage and is sitting on the top of the cage or cage door. If a child wishes to step up a quaker parrot from the cage top or door, again, teach the child to stand on a stool, ladder, or chair in order to be in a height-dominant position. This should stimulate the bird to cooperate. If the bird is nippy at the cage, the child might require the bird to step up onto a hand-held perch rather than a hand, assuming that the bird is appropriately patterned to step up to a hand-held perch as described previously. Of course, the child should also participate in step-up practice, outings, and, especially, all behavioral practices designed to balance bonding (see Balancing Bonding in Chapter Four).

A child must always be able to expect help and support from adults in providing adequate care, including annual veterinary exams, for any companion animal. Adults should also regularly examine and trim wing feathers to prevent the loss of the bird from flying-related accidents.

Maintain control of a quaker parrot on the hand by keeping the bird on the top (index) finger facing your face and maintaining eye contact.

Children should be supervised, counseled, and sometimes reminded to leave the toilet lid down so that the bird will not drown in the toilet. Children must not sleep with these friendly birds and must also be careful not to close them in drawers and doors.

Infants and Quaker Parrots

An established quaker parrot in the home might not take kindly to the introduction of a noisy rival that smells funny, has more toys, eats more often, and gets more of Mom's or Dad's attention than the bird does. A quaker parrot is more likely to grow truculent, noisy, and aggressive than to sulk, stop eating, or become depressed. These tendencies can be moderated by preparing the bird for the new baby's arrival and by providing sensitive supervision, shared attention, and positive reinforcement after the baby comes home.

Early Preparation

Preparing for a new human baby calls for increased patterning and handling a companion quaker at exactly the time when expectant humans might be naturally tempted to handle the bird less. Any time a quaker parrot receives less attention, it will naturally begin behaving in ways designed to attract attention, which might mean making more noise with its voice or with its toys. This is the worst possible time to neglect regular step-up practice.

At least three months before the baby arrives, begin introducing baby accessories into the home. Show the bird the toys for the baby and provide a similar, quaker-appropriate toy for each toy that the baby will have (at least at first). Later, toys can be periodically rotated and reintroduced to the quaker parrot as "new."

Introduce the quaker parrot to all the baby's new things, using language that lets the bird know that the baby is "connected" to the bird and to the family. Using the baby's name (or the word "Baby") and the bird's name in tandem, is often effective in establishing this behavioral tradition (pattern). When showing the baby's things to the bird, we might say, "This is Paco's baby's new toy, and this is baby's Paco's new toy."

Well in advance of the baby's arrival, begin sharing attention with the quaker parrot and a baby doll. Introduce the bird and the baby, again using the names in tandem. Cuddle and interact with the baby doll exactly as you would with the newborn, and show the bird how to interact peacefully with the new baby.

When the New Baby Comes Home

It's only natural that the new parents' attentions will be overwhelmingly directed toward the baby, but efforts should be made to find a little energy for the bird, too. The key to appropriate quaker parrot behavior during this period might be Dad. If Mom is usually the primary quaker parrot care provider, then Dad might take over those duties and forge new bonds with the bird.

This is a good time to invite friends of the bird over to visit and handle it.

This can also be an excellent opportunity for the bird to spend some time with grandparents or some other extended family. If no other alternative home is available, the quaker parrot might benefit from being boarded for the first few weeks while the human parents attach and adjust to their new offspring. Even if there is no alternative home available, the bird will benefit from excursions in the car or to other safe, indoor environments like the bank, the shopping mall, the veterinarian, or the groomer.

Whenever possible the quaker parrot should share attention and interactions with the parents in the presence of the baby. While a quaker parrot might not be actually handled at the same time a baby is being handled—for reasons of hygiene—we can talk to the bird as we talk to the baby. Modeling talking behavior for a human baby and a quaker parrot establishes a natural model/rival situation that can enhance the learning process for both human and bird.

When there's a new human infant in the home, we can prevent the development of attention-demanding behaviors in our companion quaker parrot with the generous use of *positive reinforcement* for any appropriate behavior. It's probably also a good idea to ask friends to say "Hi" to or greet the bird before coming over to coo over the baby. Continue using the bird's and the baby's names in tandem through the baby's first year to help the bird accept the child.

Introduce the quaker parrot to the new baby's toys.

Keep the Bird and the New Baby on the Same Schedule

The bird and the baby should eat, sleep, and bathe at approximately the same times. Simultaneous feeding is especially helpful in preventing the development of attention-demanding behaviors at this time. Human babies must eat frequently. Quaker parrots perceive eating as a social interaction. Feed the quaker parrot at least a little something every time you feed the baby, or serious jealousy behaviors could develop. Likewise, offer a bowl of water for the quaker to bathe in whenever bathing the baby. Of course, you must insist that the bird and the baby sleep at the same times.

Provide the quaker parrot with opportunities for wing-flapping exercise to help it to express excess energy that might develop during this exciting time in a young family's life. It's probably not a good idea to add a new quaker parrot, or any

Mommy, I'm SO Smart

I was taking a shower. It was too late for Guido to get in with me, so I put his T-bar perch between the bathroom and hallway and placed him on it.

Guido loves to imitate animal calls and sounds. When practicing his repertoire, I'll hear him say things like:

What's kitty cat say? Meow!

What's chicken say? Bruck, bruck!

What's turkey say? Gobble, gobble!

What's puppy say? Bark, bark!

What's cow say? Mooooooooo!

While in the shower, I wondered what he would say if I asked him what Bilbo (my Himalayan) said. So I asked.

Guido, what's Bilbo say?

Silence. He was thinking. Hard.

I said, *Guido, Bilbo's a kitty cat. So, what's Bilbo say.*

I instantly heard *Meow!*

I was thrilled. Could he have possibly associated Bilbo with being a kitty cat; therefore, of course, he said, *Meow?*

I waited a few moments, then asked. *Guido, what's Bilbo say?*

Again, *Meow!*

I told him what a smart bird he was. I noticed that Bilbo was sitting on the floor, almost eye-level with Guido and his perch, purring loudly.

Again, I asked the question. *Guido, what does Bilbo say?*

The answer I received this time was *Bye-bye!*

As I turned to Guido to tell him, *No, Sweetie, that's not what Bilbo....,* I noticed that Bilbo was leaving with Guido watching as he ran down the stairs. I guess his response really *was* appropriate.

Mommy was wrong.

Tena M. Marangi
Alexandria, Virginia

other pet, when a new baby has just arrived, as both creatures will require a great deal of attention.

Quaker Parrots and Other Pets

As mentioned previously, quaker parrots are probably the most social of all parrots, breeding in extremely close proximity not only to other quaker parrots, but also sharing the huge condo nest with other species such as storks, bats, geese, and opossums. It might even be said that the quaker parrot is the only parrot that "keeps pets" in the wild.

In captivity, quaker parrots may develop highly compatible relationships with other pets, as well as highly adversarial relationships. Supervising a new quaker/pet relationship, understanding quaker "culture," and reinforcing appropriate behavior for an approved neighbor is necessary to ensure complementary relationships with other pets. A carefully timed clap, squirt, or bop on the too-interested nose will pattern the other pet to avoid predatory behavior.

Like other parrots, quakers often violently defend a bond to a location or a human and jealously abuse others, including pets, that might be perceived as intruders into their territory. Locating the cage well away from traffic areas is probably crucial here, for if a particular animal rushes frequently past the quaker parrot cage, it might stimulate and pattern chasing behaviors in the bird.

Prepare to introduce a new pet into the home of an established quaker in much the same way as preparing for a new human baby, by telling the quaker parrot that the new addition is coming and by sensitively supervising their introduction. Always intervene if the quaker parrot seems to be trying to chase or attack.

Although a quaker parrot is much more likely to be killed by a dog than by a cat, caring owners know that their cats must be well socialized as kittens. Some quaker owners even feel that a cat's front claws should be removed if there is a bird in the house. In most cases this is probably unnecessary; I have seen no cases of cats killing quakers.

It is not unusual for a quaker parrot to repeatedly attack a dog. It is especially unwise to trust a quaker parrot alone with such a dog, for if the bird has abused the dog repeatedly in the past, some day that dog will defend itself, and there might not be much of the bird left.

While most quakers do well with most cats, ferrets are especially deadly to small birds. I do not recommend adding a quaker or any other small parrot to a home with a ferret.

Quakers cannot usually be trusted with either larger or smaller birds. Carefully supervise any interaction in which a larger animal interacts with smaller one, especially if the quaker parrot is the larger animal. Quaker parrots can be a threat to smaller creatures in the home such as insects, spiders, lizards, reptiles, mice, hamsters, and gerbils.

Quaker parrots enjoy socializing with other pets and must be protected from seeking the company of predatory companion animals.

Quaker parrots can be a threat to smaller creatures in the home.

Chapter Ten

Quaker Parrots in the United States

Banned in Burbank

Because laws and regulations change frequently in the United States, any published list of state regulations can be quickly out of date. Notably, quaker parrot ownership is regulated in every state. A list of states where quakers were banned, partially banned, or ownership is otherwise in question as of November 1996 appears on page 111.

It's quite difficult to obtain reliable information about the current status of these laws and regulations. Jeff Sofa of the Quaker Home

At this writing, quaker parrots are illegal in ten of the United States.

Page reports that he is often given different opinions from different sources within the same department in the same state on the same day. Many individual birds are legal in their states as a result of being "grandfathered in," that is, the birds were already in their present homes when the law or regulation was passed.

Wild Quakers in the United States

Quaker parrots have been observed as residents of the eastern United States since 1964. The 1980 edition of *Peterson Field Guides to Eastern Birds* reports that although the quaker "...has attempted to nest in a number of states from Massachusetts to Florida and west to Oklahoma, (it) will probably not become established."*

This is an interesting development considering the birds' feared

---

* Peterson, Roger Tory. *Peterson Field Guides to Eastern Birds,* Houghton Mifflin Company, 1980, page 178.

State	Law or Regulation
California	Illegal to own or sell
Connecticut	Illegal to own or sell (reportedly changing)
Georgia	Illegal to own or sell
Kansas	Illegal to own or sell (reportedly changing)
Kentucky	Illegal to own or sell
Hawaii	Illegal to own or sell
New Jersey	Illegal to own or sell
New York	Legal to own with registration and banding
Pennsylvania	Illegal to own or sell
Tennessee	Illegal to own or sell
Virginia	Legal to own with breeder or seller registration
Wyoming	Illegal to own or sell

Information Provided by Jeff Sofa/Quaker Home Page INTERNET:taz@usa.net

potential as pernicious agricultural pest and harasser and displacer of native birds. In the quaker parrot's native Argentina, the bird is considered opportunistic. The bird's native range has advanced with the ever-increasing expansion of agriculture. That is, unlike macaws, who have diminished as a result of habitat (nesting site) loss, the quaker parrot has increased numbers as a result of predation on farmlands that have replaced wild habitat.

Some insight into the quaker parrot's failure to expand in the United States might be provided by David Wright, a CompuServe regular who has studied feral quakers in Connecticut and on the eastern coast of the United States. Wright suggests that feral quaker parrots survive in areas where there is year-round food, an abundance of large trees, and prox-imity to a large body of fresh water. He observes that quakers do not leave the immediate area from which they were fledged, and therefore have not proliferated as feared in areas where they have become a fixture.

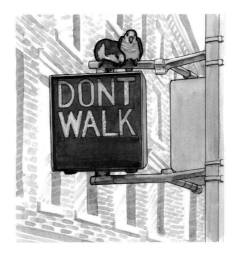

Quaker parrots are well established in several urban areas in the eastern United States.

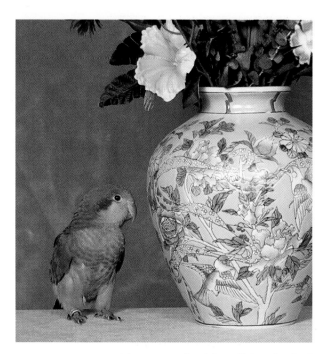

Handfed domestic quakers have little or no chance of surviving outdoors.

apparently have not produced off-spring.

I have not yet seen a hand-fed domestic bird with the necessary skills to survive outdoors. Even the attempted reintroduction of domestic thick-billed parrots specially trained to live wild has demonstrated that most domestically raised parrots probably have little or no chance of surviving wild. In my experience, when hand-fed quakers accidentally fly away, they usually wind up going to a human rather than seeking out-door food and water sources.

From many years of recapturing feral quakers in Colorado, I believe that most of the birds living wild in this country are escaped, wild-caught, imported birds. The quaker parrot has not been legally imported into the United States since 1993. Because of the captured quaker parrot's relatively low market value, I doubt that smugglers are bringing them into the United States illegally.

I have watched free-flying "pairs" of quaker parrots that make loosely woven temporary nests in Colorado. Even though some of these birds have long survived outdoors, they

Chapter Eleven
The Companion Quaker in Brazil

São Paulo, Brazil is one of the world's most populous cities, home to ten million humans and growing. I have seen it once—in the movie, *Pixote*—a view of beachside skyscrapers closely set against a backdrop of mountains. According to Josoph DeAlmaioa, a native Brazilian who emigrated to Colorado, the Portuguese-speaking citizens of São Paulo are crazy about talking quaker parrots.

Mr. DeAlmaioa is the youngest of seven children. Born in São Paulo, he spent most of his early childhood in the Amazon rain forest where his father owned a store.

He reports that the quaker parrot is extremely common both as ferals in rural southern Brazil and as pets in the densely populated cities to the north. He also says that quakers may be "the most common pet" in São Paulo where they are sometimes kept as individual, one-owner birds, or with shared ownership as a "community bird" living in the patio or common room of an apartment complex.

"That bird is a very good talker," Mr. DeAlmaioa laughs. "They have contests on television every year, and people know the names of the famous good talking quakers and their owners. The birds are usually taught jokes—usually, dirty jokes." Now Mr. DeAlmaioa is blushing.

Quakers are worth little at country fairs or markets in the rural south of Brazil, where a basket of babies offered for a very low price might go unsold. Wild-caught babies can bring higher prices in the northern cities where only a few birds are bred domestically. Industrious dealers sometimes bring the birds north to São Paulo by truckload.

Oh, just one other thing—Mr. DeAlmaioa also says that if you have a quaker parrot in the house, "You can never lie to your spouse." According to Brazilian folklore, the bird will tell on you!

Glossary

Please note that the following definitions set forth the meanings of these words as they are used specifically in this text. They are not intended to be full and complete definitions.

aggression: hostile nipping, biting, or chasing.

ailanthus: trees of heaven, weed tree common in older urban cities in the United States. So named for a Moluccan word meaning, "tree that grows up to the sky." Soft, easy to grip branches well-suited to quaker parrot perches.

allofeeding: mutual feeding or simulated mutual feeding. One of several behaviors related to breeding.

allopreening: mutual preening or simulated mutual preening, for example, a human scratching a parrot's neck.

anthropomorphizing: ascribing human attributes to a non-human thing.

baby days: a young parrot's first, impressionable weeks in the new home, an idyllic period before the baby bird's instincts for independence, dominance, and exploration develop. *See also:* honeymoon period.

band: coded metal device placed around a bird's leg for identification purposes.

behavioral environment: behavioral conditions, especially redundant or habitual behaviors, present in the bird and in individuals around the bird.

bite: use of the parrot's beak in a manner intended to cause damage or injury.

bite zone: area in front of the bird's beak in which the hand can easily be bitten but not easily stepped on (described on pages 18–19).

blood feather: unopened immature feather which is completely or partially covered by a bluish/white membrane indicating that the feather is currently supplied with blood.

bonding: the connection with another bird, a human, object, or location which a bird exhibits and defends.

breeding-related behaviors: behaviors with a source related to breeding habits in the wild such as arranging, (nest-building), allopreening, allofeeding, masturbating, copulating, and aggression at the nest site (cage).

cataract: an abnormally opaque lens in the eye, usually restricting sight.

cavity-breeding: describes breeding-related chewing behaviors of parrots other than quaker parrots.

chasing: to drive away by pursuing.

command: an order or instruction given by a dominant individual.

covert: a layer of covering feathers as in the gray and green feathers covering the bird's down.

developmental period: a behavioral period wherein the bird's instincts for dominance, independence, and aggression are first manifest. *See also:* terrible twos.

dominance: control, enforcing individual will over others.

down: the small fuzzy feathers next to the body that are normally covered by coverts.

drama: any activity that brings an excited response either positive or negative.

earthquake: a behavioral correction performed during step-up practice. *See also:* Wobble Correction (page 21).

eye contact: the act of maintaining eye-to-eye gaze.

flock/flock mates: as it applies to a companion bird, human companions sharing a home with a captive parrot.

forage: the search for food.

gathering: the process of hoarding food for future use.

good hand/bad hand: a behavioral technique designed to distract a bird from biting.

grooming: the process of having the companion parrot's wing feathers trimmed, nails cut or filed, and, if necessary, beak shaped.

habit: redundant behavior that has become a fixed part of the bird's conduct.

hand-fed: a parrot that as a neonate was fed by humans rather than birds

handling techniques: methods used by humans to stimulate and maintain successful tactile interactions with companion parrots.

harvesting: removing ripe fruits or vegetables so that they may provide future forage. *See also:* gathering.

honeymoon period: a young parrot's first, impressionable weeks in the new home, an idyllic period before the bird's instinct for dominance and exploration develop. *See also:* baby days.

independence: improvising and enjoying self-rewarding behaviors.

juvenile: immature behaviors unrelated to nesting or breeding.

language: a method of verbal communication wherein multiple individuals use the same sounds or groups of sounds to convey the same meanings.

mandible: the beak, horny protuberance with which the bird bites.

manzanita: commercially available hardwood branches, that in small sizes are suitable for quaker parrot perches.

mate: the individual to whom a quaker parrot is primarily bonded.

model: a learning process by which one individual copies behavior from another individual.

molt: the cyclical shedding and replacing of feathers.

neonate: a baby parrot that cannot yet eat food independently.

nest/nesting: the act of constructing a structure for the purpose of reproduction.

nest box: a human constructed box for bird nesting.

nipping: an accidental, unintentional, or non-aggressive bite not intended to cause damage.

parakeet: a parrot with a long, graduated tail.

parrot: a bird with a notched upper mandible, a mallet shaped tongue, and four toes (two facing front and two facing back).

patterning: stimulating an individual to repeat behaviors through the process of repeatedly drilling the behavior.

There's an old saying, "Live as though you could sell the family parrot." (A quaker parrot will repeat what it hears.)

pecking order: the hierarchy of dominance within a group of birds or their companions.

polymer fume fever: the condition that can kill a bird that is exposed to fumes from Teflon heated to 500°F.

preen: to groom the feathers, as with "combing" and "zipping" them with the beak.

prompt: a cue, here used for the physical cue to cause the bird to step up.

psittacine: any parrot.

quaking: palsy-like feeding response of baby quakers that may be occasionally repeated in compromised or courting adults.

quarantine: enforced isolation for the prevention of disease transmission.

recapture: to apprehend or recover possession of a parrot that has flown away.

regurgitate: voluntary or involuntary production of partially digested food from the crop. *See also:* allofeeding.

reinforce: process of rewarding a behavior that we wish to become habitual.

rescue: fortuitous removal from frightening circumstances.

rival: a competitor, one who competes for reinforcement or reward.

roaming: unsupervised explorations away from approved cage or play areas.

roost: the place where a bird usually sleeps.

self-rewarding behavior: an activity that is enacted solely for the pleasure of doing it.

sexual behavior: self-rewarding breeding-related behavior.

sexual maturity: the period during which breeding-related behaviors become prominent in the bird's over-all behavior.

signaling: anything that warns, alerts, or telegraphs an intention or apparent intention which might generate a reaction.

status: positioning related to dominance within the pecking order.

step-up: practice of giving the step-up command with the expectation that the bird will perform the behavior.

stress: any stimulus, especially fear or pain, that inhibits normal psychological, physical, or behavioral balance.

subspecies: a subdivision of species, especially by color or geographical characteristics.

substrata: material placed in the bottom of the bird's cage or play area to contain mess and droppings.

sumac: a small, sparsely branching weed tree found in pastures and adjoining land throughout most of the United States. Sumac is not poisonous, but rather is a common food source for many native species of birds. It is suitable for use as quaker parrot perches and toys.

terrible twos: a behavioral period wherein the bird's instincts for dominance, independence, and aggression are first manifest. *See also:* developmental period.

tool: an implement that is manipulated to accomplish a particular function.

toxin: any substance that causes illness or death through exposure to it.

toy: any tool for producing self-rewarding behavior.

trap: a device used to recapture a free-flying bird.

vocabulary: words or elements comprising a language.

window of opportunity: a finite period during which something can be accomplished, a period of time during which behavior can be changed.

wobble correction: a behavioral correction performed during step-up practice (see page 21). *See also:* earthquake.

Useful Addresses and Literature

Books

Athan, *Guide to a Well-Behaved Parrot,* Barron's Educational Series, Hauppauge, NY, 1993.

Burgmann, *Feeding Your Pet Bird,* Barron's Educational Series, Hauppauge, NY, 1993.

Hubbard, *The New Parrot Training Handbook*, Hubbard, Fremont, CA, 1997.

Jordan, *The Quaker Handbook,* Jordan Ent., Evansville, IN, 1993.

Ritchie, Harrison & Harrison, *Avian Medicine, Principles and Application,* Wingers Publishing, Inc., Lake Worth, FL, 1994.

Magazines

Bird Talk Magazine
P.O. Box 6050
Mission Viejo, CA 92690

Birds USA
P.O. Box 6050
Mission Viejo, CA 92690

The Quaker News
P.O. Box 609
Fruitland Park, FL 34731-0609

Pet Bird Report
2236 Mariner Square Drive #35
Alameda, CA 94501-1059

Internet Resource

Quaker Home Page,
INTERNET:taz@usa.net

Organizations

American Federation of Aviculture
P.O. Box 56218
Phoenix, AZ 85079

Index